Bond

Non-verbal Reasoning

Assessment Papers

11⁺–12⁺ years
Book 1

Alison Primrose

Nelson Thornes

Text © Alison Primrose 2004, 2007
Original illustrations © Nelson Thornes Ltd 2007

The right of Alison Primrose to be identified as author of this work has been asserted by
her in accordance with the Copyright, Designs and Patents Act 1988.

All rights reserved. No part of this publication may be reproduced or transmitted in any
form or by any means, electronic or mechanical, including photocopy, recording or any
information storage and retrieval system, without permission in writing from the
publisher or under licence from the Copyright Licensing Agency Limited, of Saffron
House, 6–10 Kirby Street, London, EC1N 8TS.

Any person who commits any unauthorised act in relation to this publication may be
liable to criminal prosecution and civil claims for damages.

First published in 2004 by:
Nelson Thornes Ltd

Second edition published in 2007 by:
Nelson Thornes Ltd
Delta Place
27 Bath Road
CHELTENHAM
GL53 7TH
United Kingdom

12 13 14 / 10 9 8 7 6 5 4 3 2 1

A catalogue record for this book is available from the British Library

ISBN 978 1 4085 1690 4

Illustrations by Bede Illustration
Page make-up by Wearset Ltd

Printed and bound in Egypt by Sahara Printing Company

Before you get started

What is Bond?

This book is part of the Bond Assessment Papers series for non-verbal reasoning, which provides a **thorough and progressive course in non-verbal reasoning** from ages six to twelve. It builds up non-verbal reasoning skills from book to book over the course of the series. Bond's non-verbal reasoning resources are ideal preparation for the 11+ and other secondary school selection exams.

How does the scope of this book match real exam content?

Non-verbal Reasoning 11+-12+ Book 1 and *Book 2* are the advanced Bond 11+ books. Each paper is **pitched at a level above a typical 11+ exam,** providing greater challenges and stretching skills further. The papers practise a wide range of questions drawn from the four distinct groups of non-verbal reasoning question types: identifying shapes, missing shapes, rotating shapes, coded shapes and logic. The papers are fully in line with 11+ and other selective exams for this age group but are designed to practise **a wider variety of skills and question types** than most other practice papers so that children are always challenged to think – and don't get bored repeating the same question type again and again. We believe that variety is the key to effective learning. It helps children 'think on their feet' and cope with the unexpected: it is surprising how often children come out of non-verbal reasoning exams having met question types they have not seen before.

What does the book contain?

- **6 papers** – each one contains 60 questions.

- **Tutorial links throughout** – 📖 – this icon appears in the margin next to the questions. It indicates links to the relevant section in *How to do ... 11+ Non-verbal Reasoning*, our invaluable subject guide that offers explanations and practice for all core question types.

- **Scoring devices** – there is a score box at the end of each test and a Progress Chart on page 68. The chart is a visual and motivating way for children to see how they are doing. It also turns the score into a percentage that can help decide what to do next.

- **Next Steps Planner** – advice on what to do after finishing the papers can be found on the inside back cover.

- **Answers** – located in an easily-removed central pull-out section.

How can you use this book?

One of the great strengths of Bond Assessment Papers is their flexibility. They can be used at home, in school and by tutors to:

- set **timed formal practice** tests – allow about 45 minutes per paper in line with standard 11+ demands. Reduce the suggested time limit by five minutes to practise working at speed.

- provide **bite-sized chunks** for regular practice

- **highlight strengths and weaknesses** in the core skills

- identify **individual needs**

- set **homework**

- follow **a complete 11+ preparation strategy** alongside *The Parents' Guide to the 11+* (see below).

It is best to start at the beginning and work through the papers in order. If you are using the book as part of a careful run-in to the 11+, we suggest that you also have two other essential Bond resources close at hand:

How to do . . . 11+ Non-verbal Reasoning: the subject guide that explains all the question types practised in this book. Use the cross-reference icons to find the relevant sections.

The Parents' Guide to the 11+: the step-by-step guide to the whole 11+ experience. It clearly explains the 11+ process, provides guidance on how to assess children, helps you to set complete action plans for practice and explains how you can use the *Non-verbal Reasoning 11+-12+ Book 1* and *Book 2* as part of a strategic run-in to the exam.

See the inside front cover for more details of these books.

What does a score mean and how can it be improved?

It is unfortunately impossible to guarantee that a child will pass the 11+ exam if they achieve a certain score on any practice book or paper. Success on the day depends on a host of factors, including the scores of the other children sitting the test. However, we can give some guidance on what a score indicates and how to improve it.

If children colour in the Progress Chart on page 68, this will give an idea of present performance in percentage terms. The Next Steps Planner inside the back cover will help you to decide what to do next to help a child progress. It is always valuable to go over wrong answers with children. If they are having trouble with any particular question type, follow the tutorial links to *How to do . . . 11+ Non-verbal Reasoning* for step-by-step explanations and further practice.

Don't forget the website . . . !

Visit www.bond11plus.co.uk for lots of advice, information and suggestions on everything to do with Bond, the 11+ and helping children to do their best, and exams.

Paper 1

Which pattern on the right belongs in the group on the left? Circle the letter.

Example

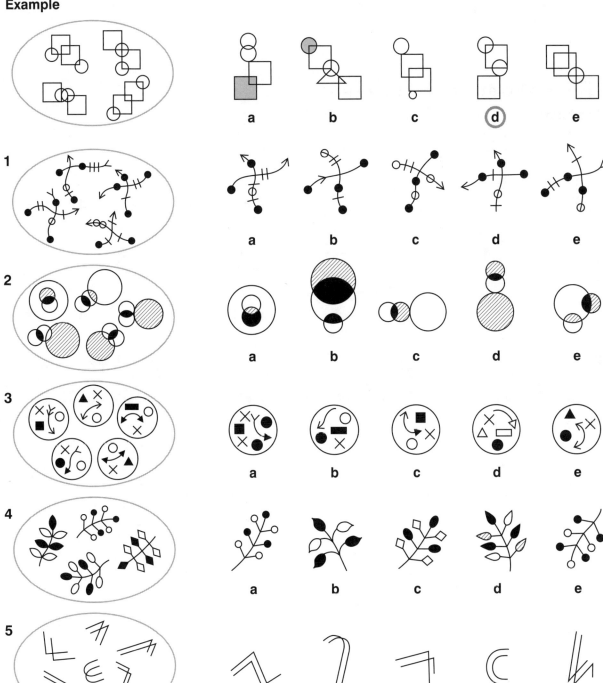

6

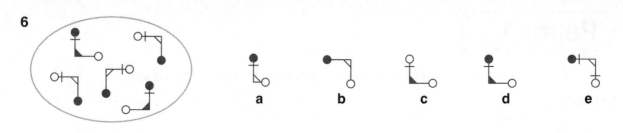

B 4 Which one comes next? Circle the letter.

Example

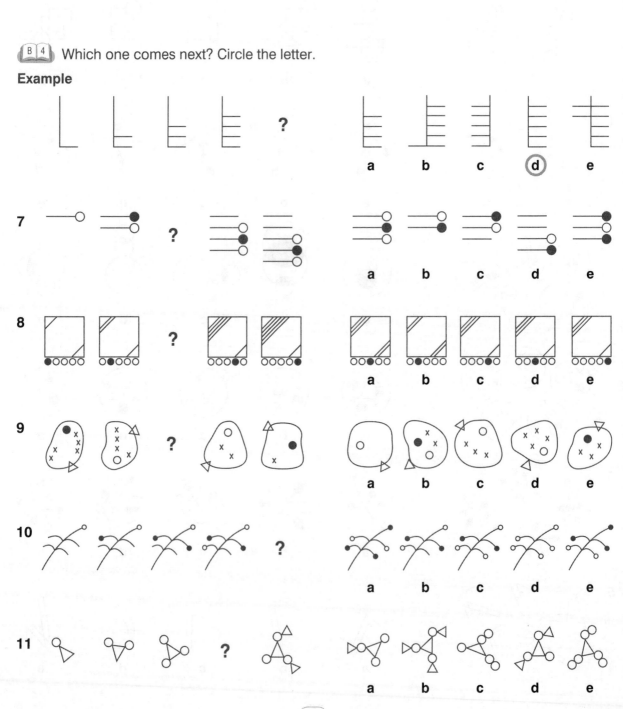

7

8

9

10

11

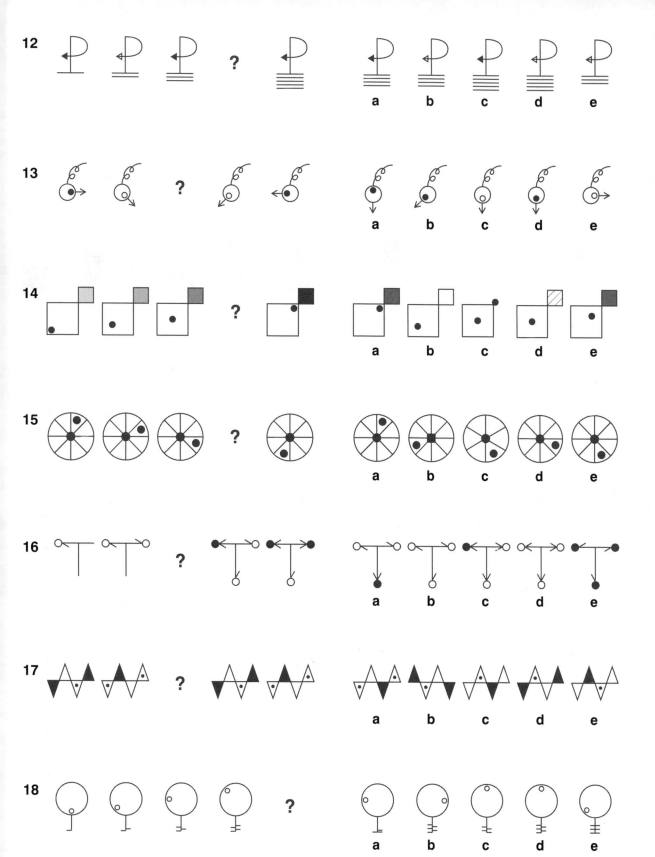

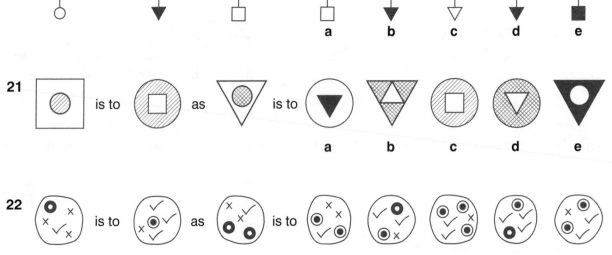

B 3 Which shape or pattern on the right completes the second pair in the same way as the first pair? Circle the letter.

Example

is to ... as ... is to

a   b   c   **d**   e

19   is to ... as ... is to

a   b   c   d   e

20   is to ... as ... is to

a   b   c   d   e

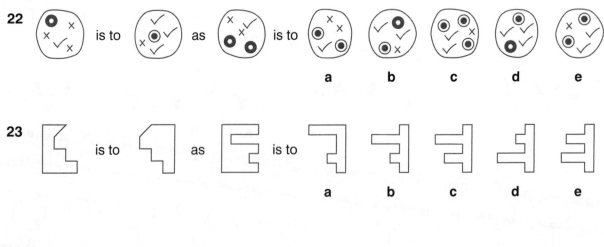

21   is to ... as ... is to

a   b   c   d   e

22   is to ... as ... is to

a   b   c   d   e

23   is to ... as ... is to

a   b   c   d   e

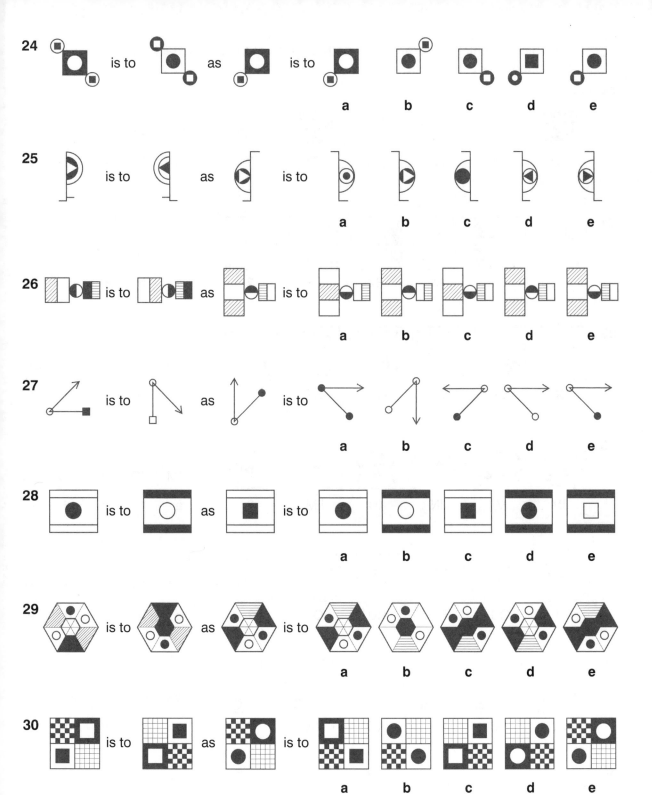

Which code matches the shape or pattern given at the end of each line?
Circle the letter.

Example

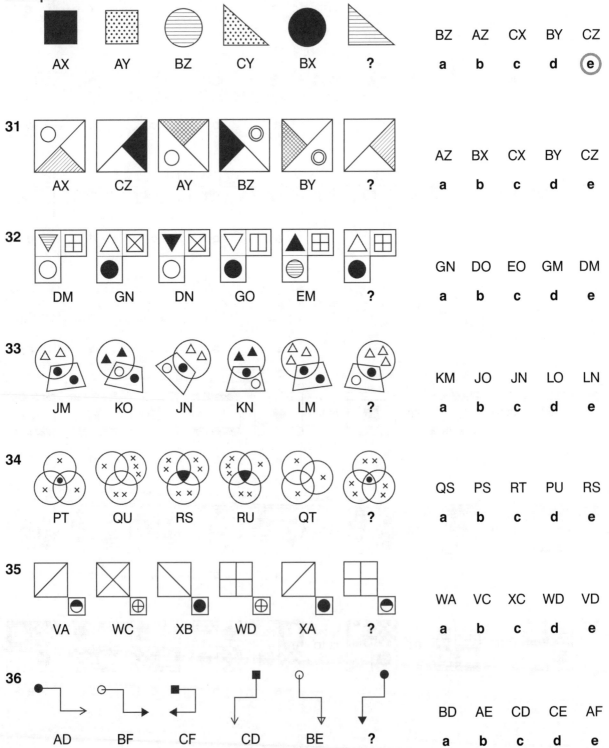

| | | | | | | BZ | AZ | CX | BY | CZ |
| | | | | | | a | b | c | d | (e) |

AX   AY   BZ   CY   BX   ?

31

AX   CZ   AY   BZ   BY   ?

AZ   BX   CX   BY   CZ
a   b   c   d   e

32

DM   GN   DN   GO   EM   ?

GN   DO   EO   GM   DM
a   b   c   d   e

33

JM   KO   JN   KN   LM   ?

KM   JO   JN   LO   LN
a   b   c   d   e

34

PT   QU   RS   RU   QT   ?

QS   PS   RT   PU   RS
a   b   c   d   e

35

VA   WC   XB   WD   XA   ?

WA   VC   XC   WD   VD
a   b   c   d   e

36

AD   BF   CF   CD   BE   ?

BD   AE   CD   CE   AF
a   b   c   d   e

Which is the odd one out? Circle the letter.

Example

37

38

39

40

41

42

Which cube cannot be made from the given net? Circle the letter.

Example

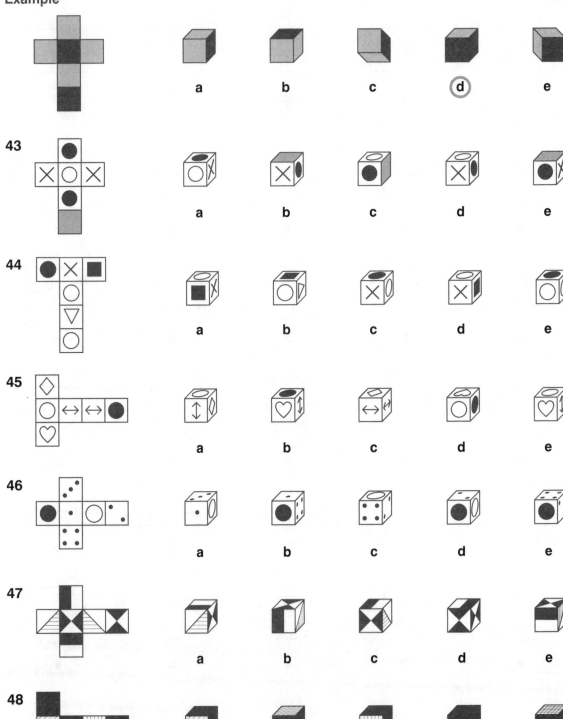

43

44

45

46

47

48

B 7 Which shape on the right is the reflection of the shape given on the left? Circle the letter.

Example

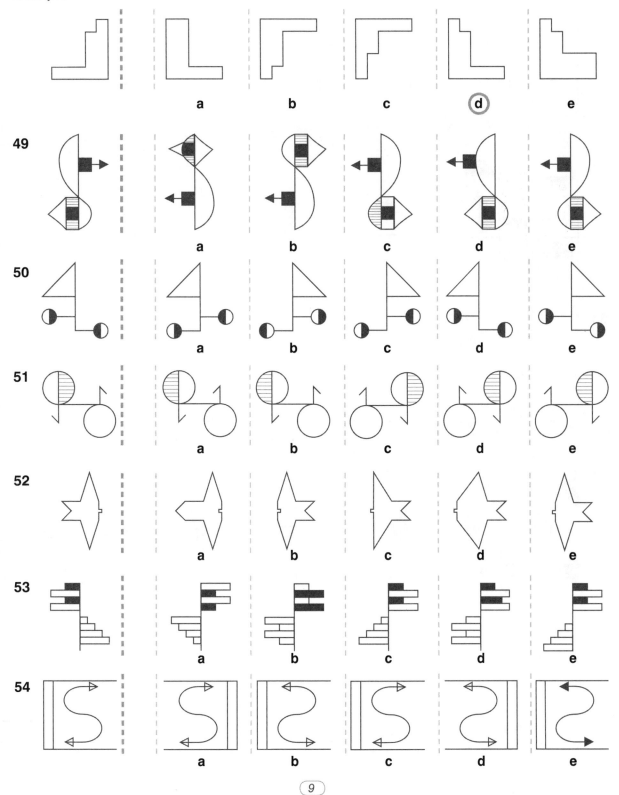

Which shape or pattern completes the larger square? Circle the letter.

Example

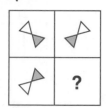

  a

  b

  c

  (d)

  e

55

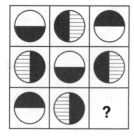

a   b   c   d   e

56

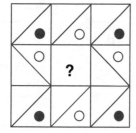

a   b   c   d   e

57

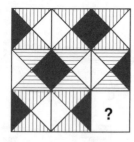

a   b   c   d   e

58

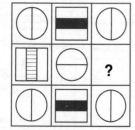

a   b   c   d   e

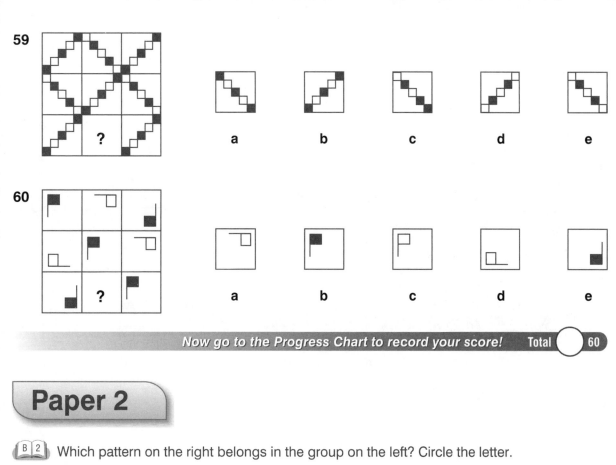

59

| | | | | |
|a|b|c|d|e|

60

| | | | | |
|a|b|c|d|e|

Now go to the Progress Chart to record your score! **Total** 60

Paper 2

B 2 Which pattern on the right belongs in the group on the left? Circle the letter.

Example

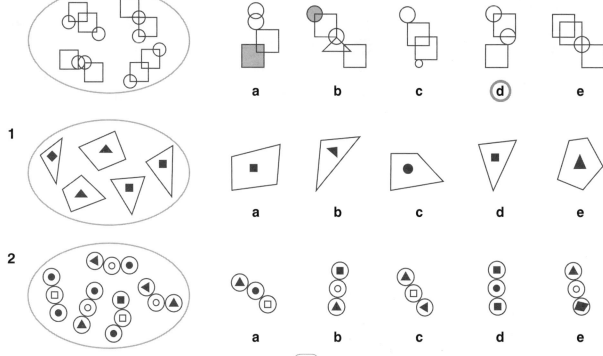

| | | | | |
|a|b|c|**d**|e|

1

| | | | | |
|a|b|c|d|e|

2

| | | | | |
|a|b|c|d|e|

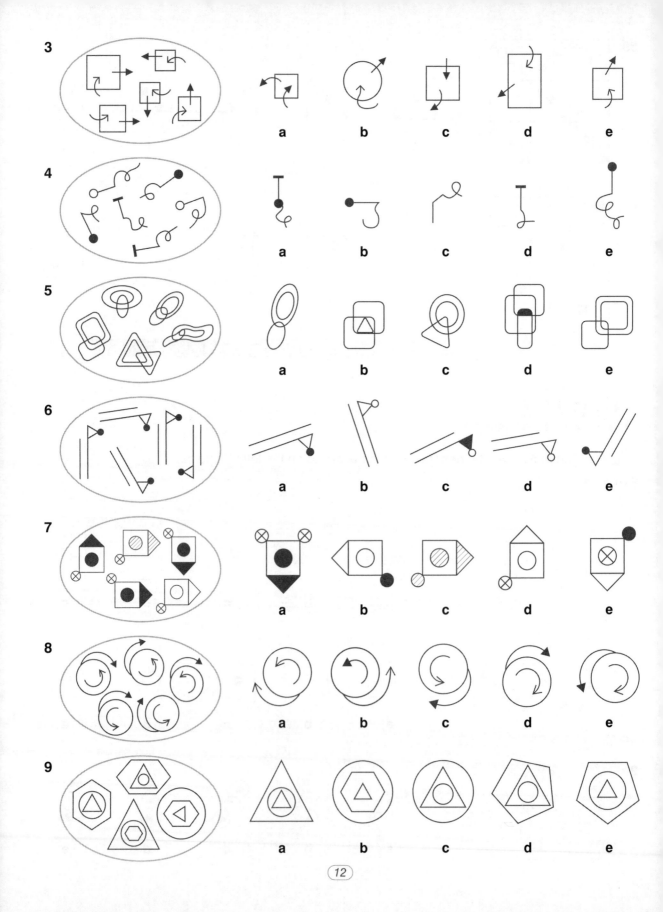

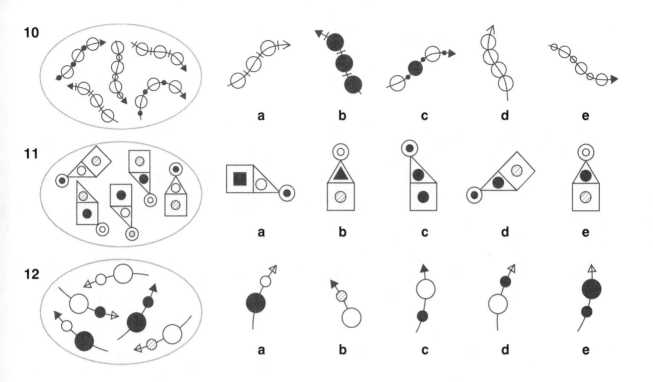

10

11

12

B 4 Which one comes next. Circle the letter.

Example

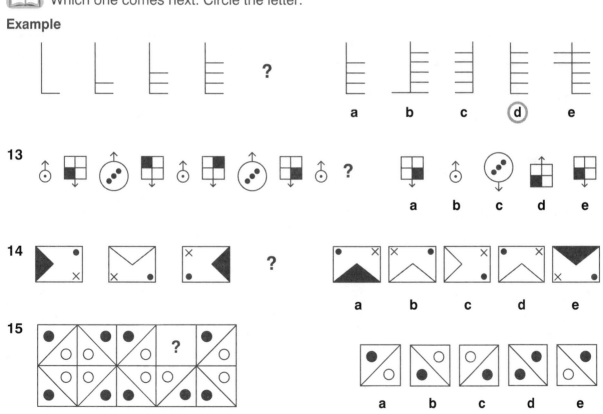

13

14

15

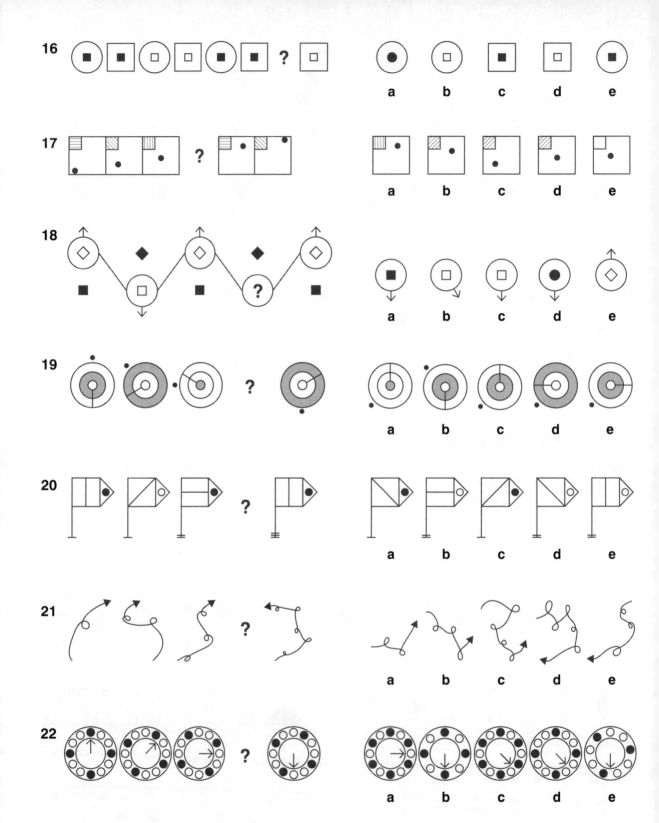

23

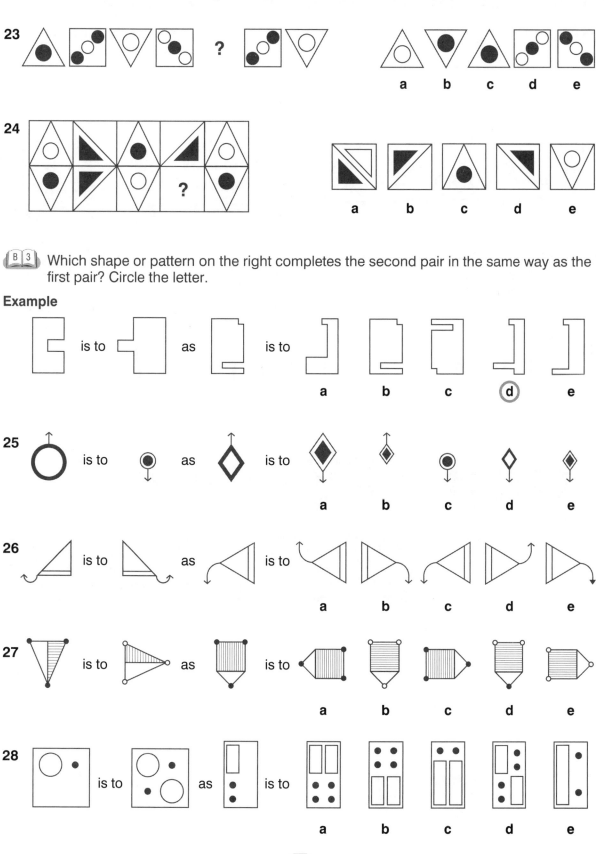

24

B 3 Which shape or pattern on the right completes the second pair in the same way as the first pair? Circle the letter.

Example

is to ... as ... is to

a b c d e

25

is to ... as ... is to

a b c d e

26

is to ... as ... is to

a b c d e

27

is to ... as ... is to

a b c d e

28

is to ... as ... is to

a b c d e

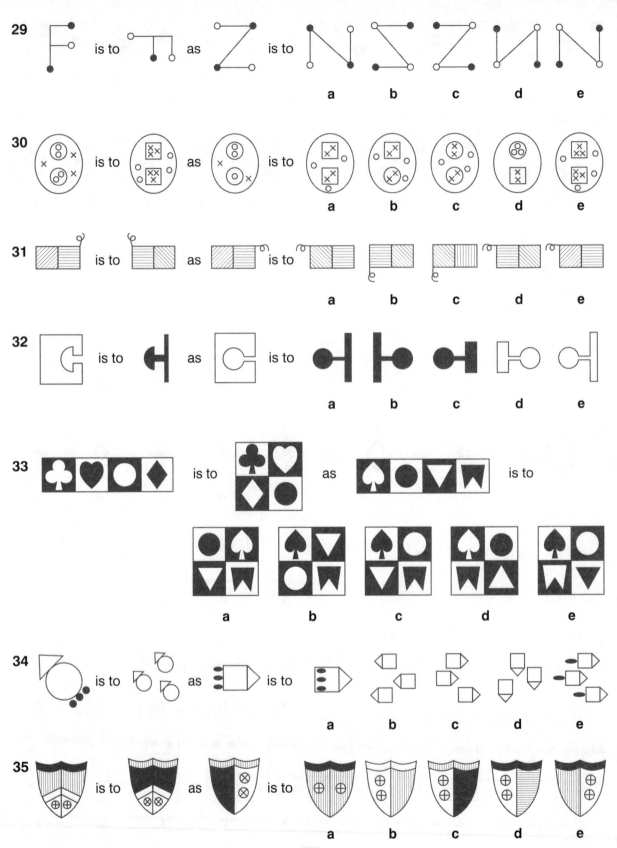

36

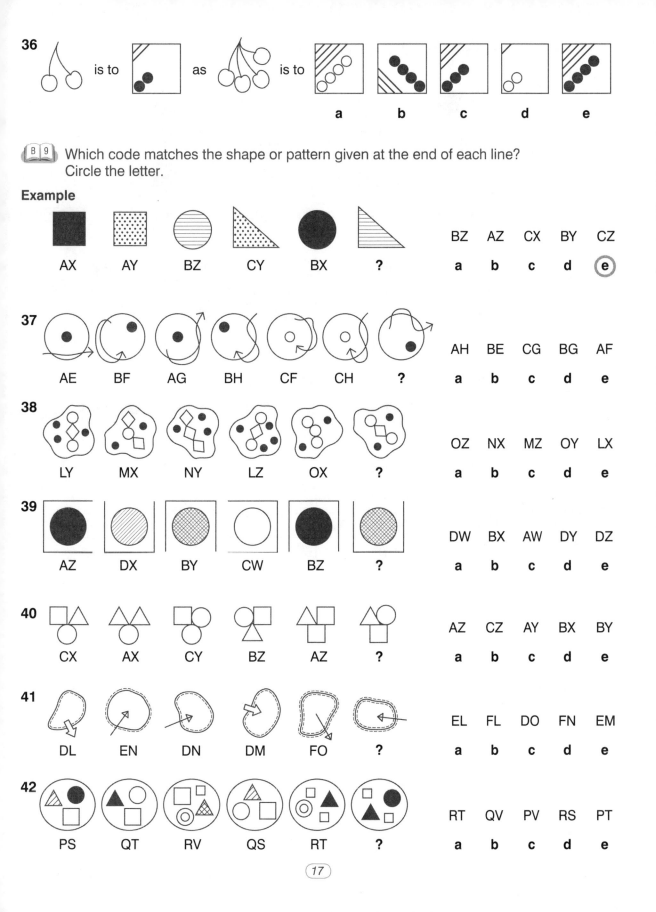

is to [ ] as [ ] is to

a   b   c   d   e

B 9 Which code matches the shape or pattern given at the end of each line?
Circle the letter.

Example

AX   AY   BZ   CY   BX   ?

BZ   AZ   CX   BY   CZ
a   b   c   d   e

37

AE   BF   AG   BH   CF   CH   ?

AH   BE   CG   BG   AF
a   b   c   d   e

38

LY   MX   NY   LZ   OX   ?

OZ   NX   MZ   OY   LX
a   b   c   d   e

39

AZ   DX   BY   CW   BZ   ?

DW   BX   AW   DY   DZ
a   b   c   d   e

40

CX   AX   CY   BZ   AZ   ?

AZ   CZ   AY   BX   BY
a   b   c   d   e

41

DL   EN   DN   DM   FO   ?

EL   FL   DO   FN   EM
a   b   c   d   e

42

PS   QT   RV   QS   RT   ?

RT   QV   PV   RS   PT
a   b   c   d   e

17

Which net makes the cube? Circle the letter.

Example

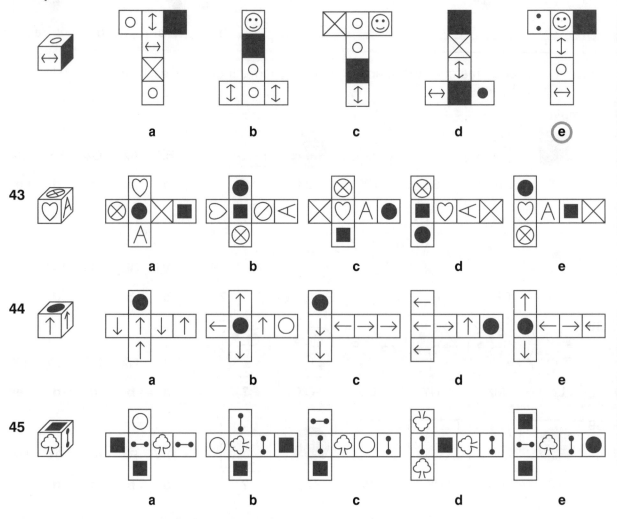

Example

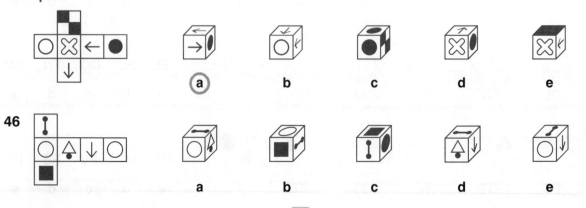

47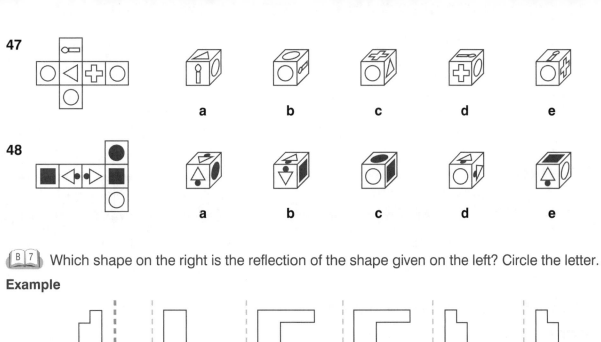

a   b   c   d   e

48

a   b   c   d   e

Which shape on the right is the reflection of the shape given on the left? Circle the letter.

Example

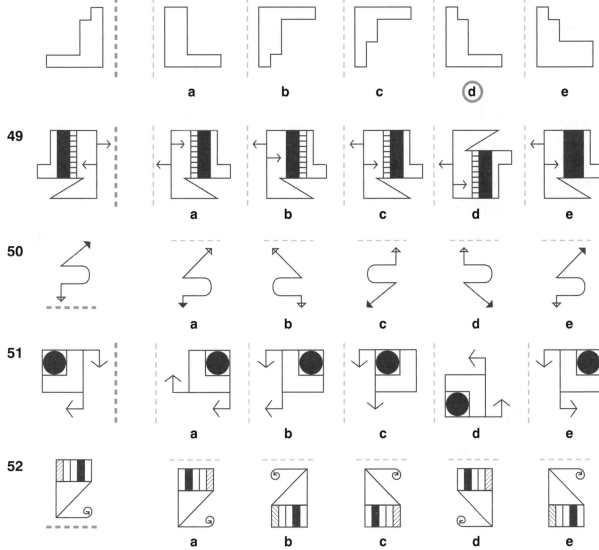

a   b   c   (d)   e

49

a   b   c   d   e

50

a   b   c   d   e

51

a   b   c   d   e

52

a   b   c   d   e

53

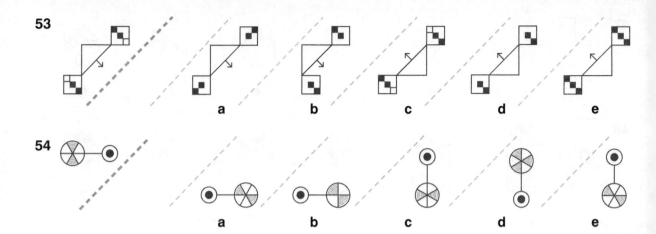

a b c d e

54

a b c d e

Which shape or pattern completes the larger square? Circle the letter.

Example

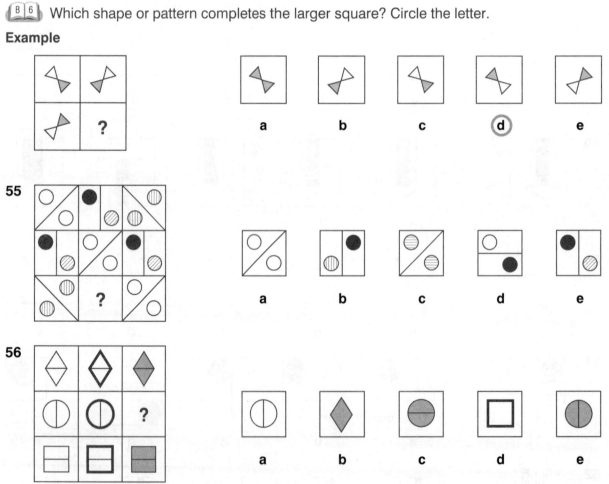

a b c (d) e

55

a b c d e

56

a b c d e

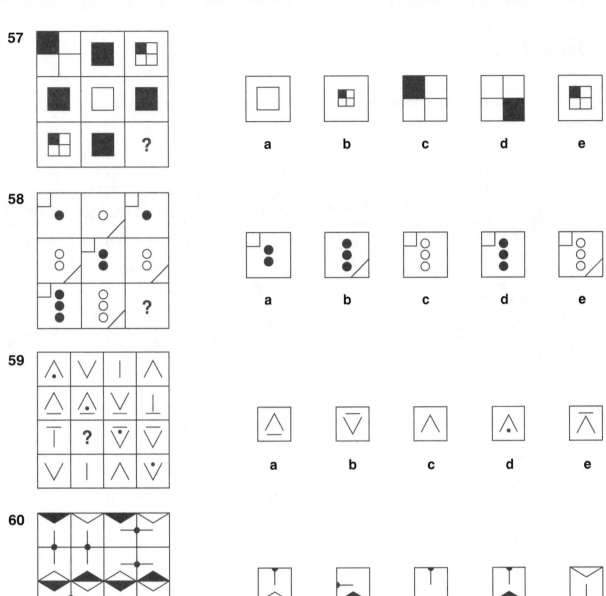

Now go to the Progress Chart to record your score! Total 60

Paper 3

B 2 Which pattern on the right belongs in the group on the left? Circle the letter.

Example

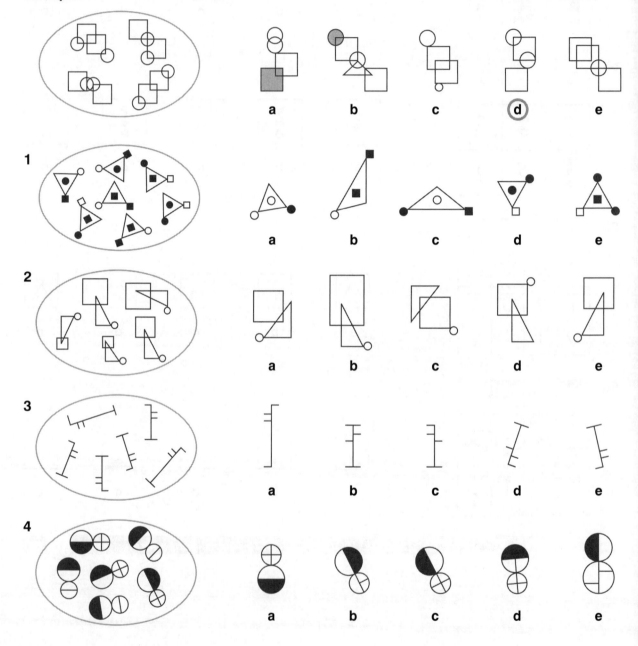

a   b   c   **d**   e

1   a   b   c   d   e

2   a   b   c   d   e

3   a   b   c   d   e

4   a   b   c   d   e

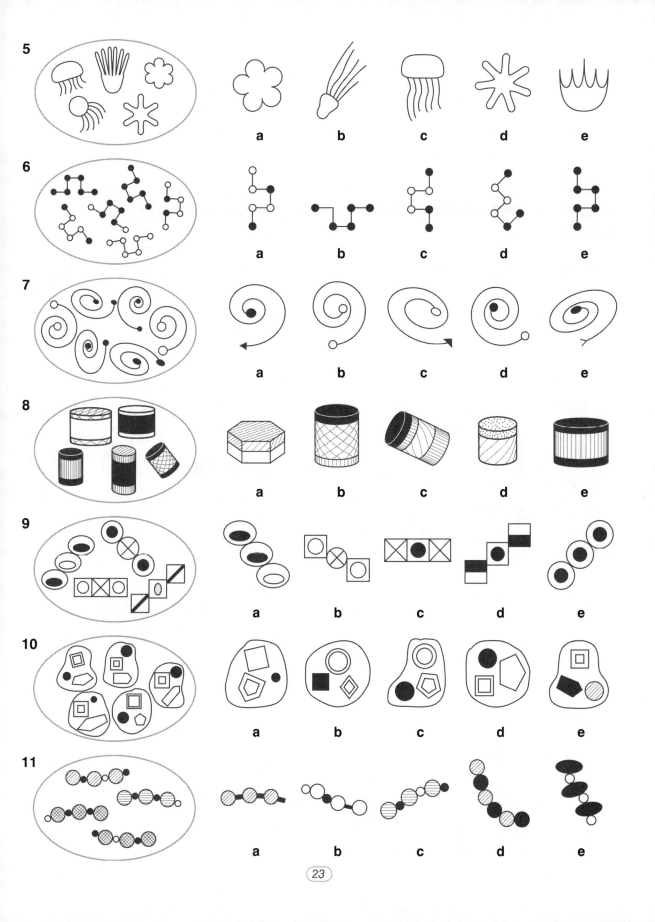

12

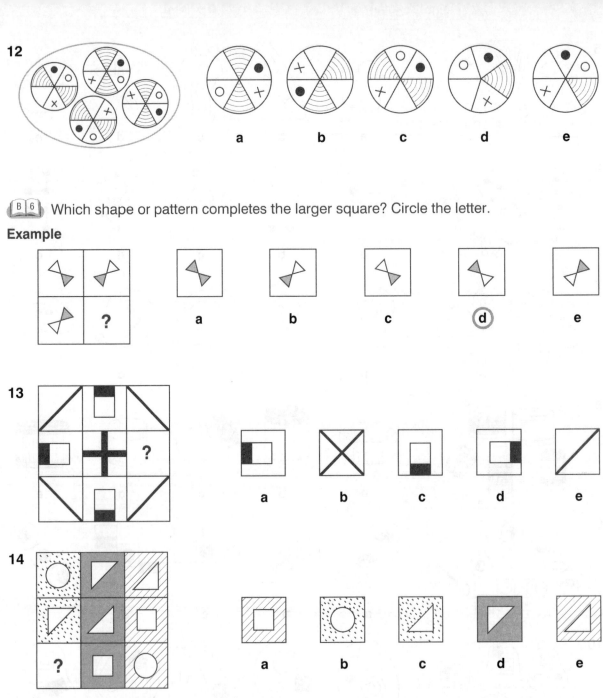

Which shape or pattern completes the larger square? Circle the letter.

Example

13

14

15

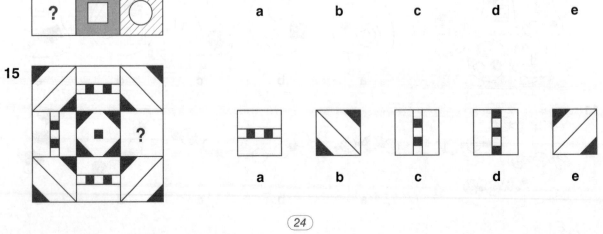

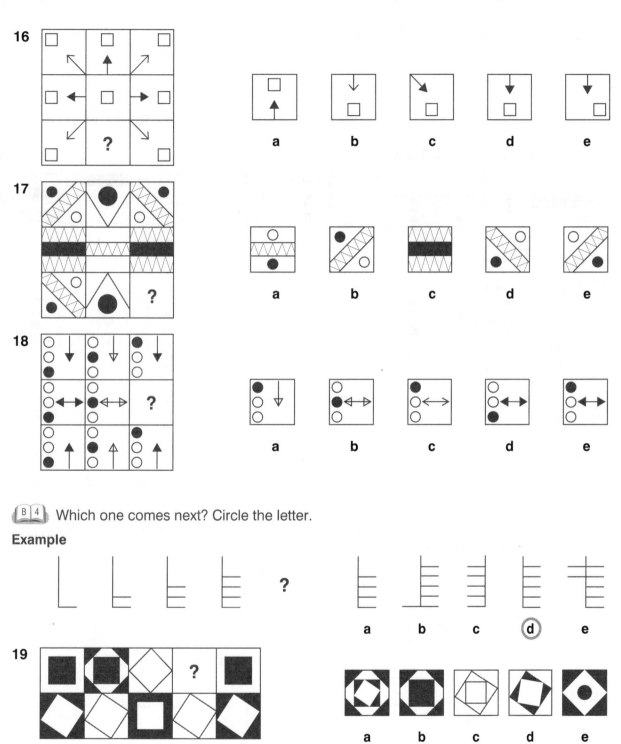

16

17

18

Which one comes next? Circle the letter.

Example

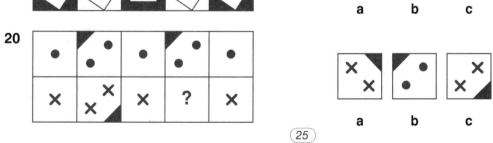

a   b   c   (d)   e

19

a   b   c   d   e

20

a   b   c   d   e

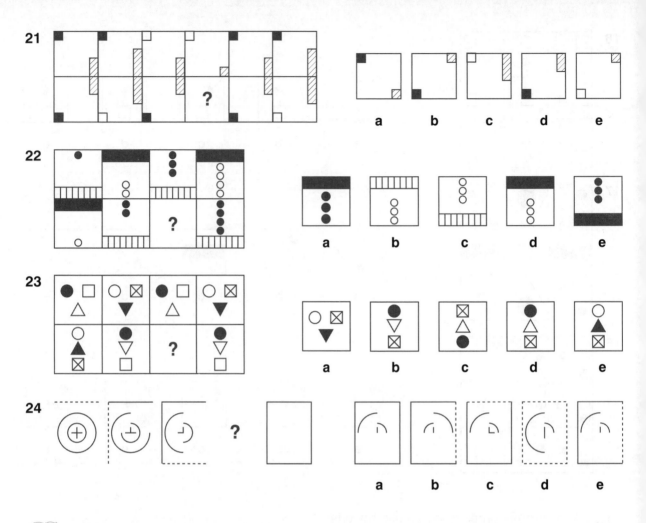

21

a b c d e

22

a b c d e

23

a b c d e

24

? a b c d e

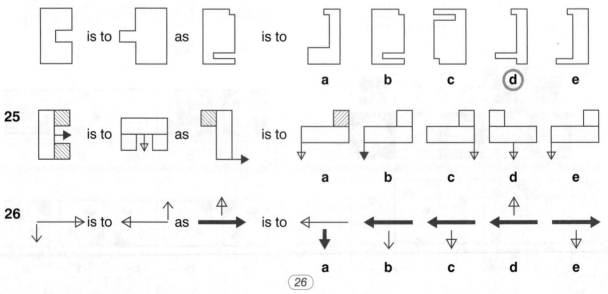

B 3 Which shape or pattern on the right completes the second pair in the same way as the first pair? Circle the letter.

Example

is to □ as □ is to

a b c d e

25

is to as is to

a b c d e

26

is to as is to

a b c d e

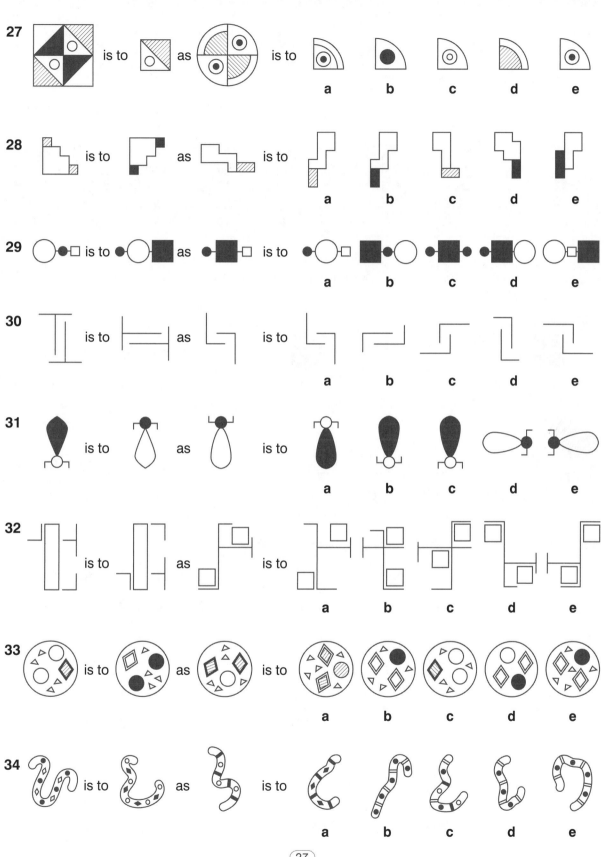

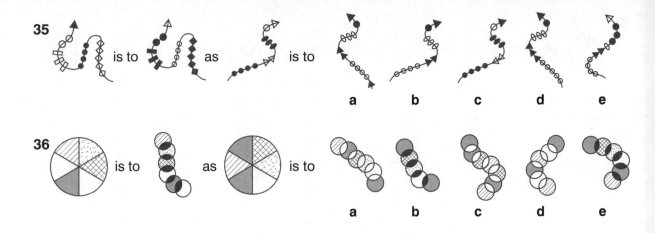

35 is to as is to

a b c d e

36 is to as is to

a b c d e

 Which code matches the shape or pattern given at the end of each line? Circle the letter.

Example

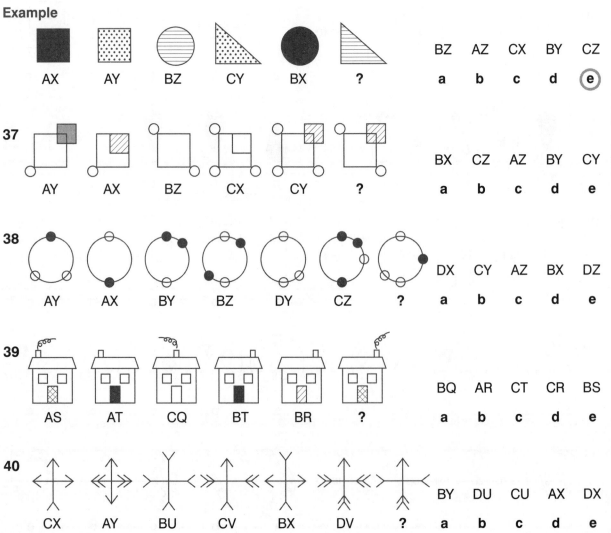

| | | | | | | | BZ | AZ | CX | BY | CZ |
| | | | | | | | a | b | c | d | (e) |

AX AY BZ CY BX ?

37

BX CZ AZ BY CY
a b c d e

AY AX BZ CX CY ?

38

DX CY AZ BX DZ
a b c d e

AY AX BY BZ DY CZ ?

39

BQ AR CT CR BS
a b c d e

AS AT CQ BT BR ?

40

BY DU CU AX DX
a b c d e

CX AY BU CV BX DV ?

28

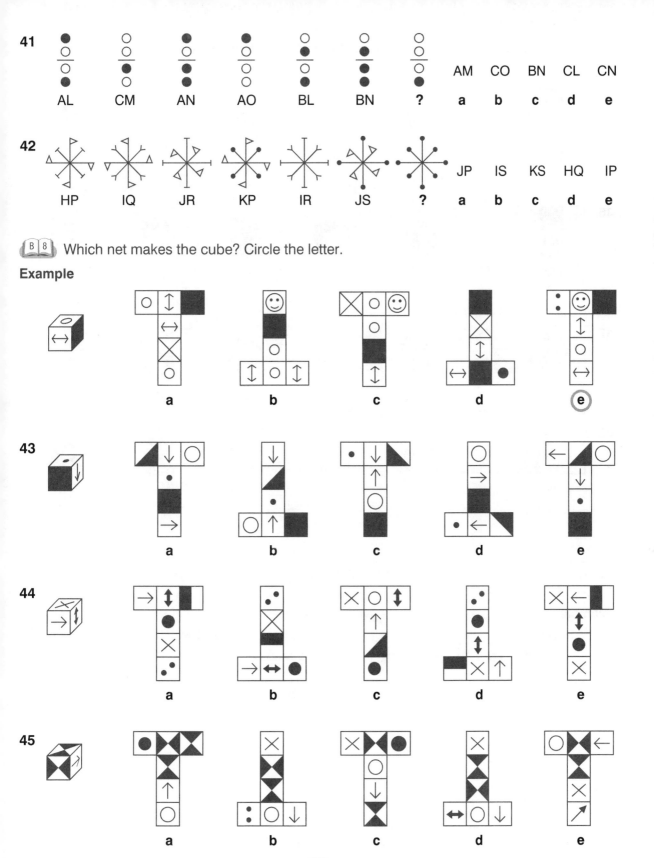

41

AM CO BN CL CN
a b c d e

42

JP IS KS HQ IP
a b c d e

B 8 Which net makes the cube? Circle the letter.

Example

a b c d (e)

43

a b c d e

44

a b c d e

45

a b c d e

Which cube can be made from the given net? Circle the letter.

Example

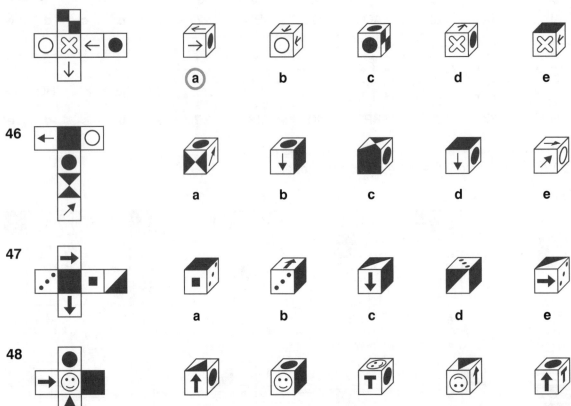

46

47

48

Which shape or pattern is made when the first two shapes or patterns are put together? Circle the letter.

Example

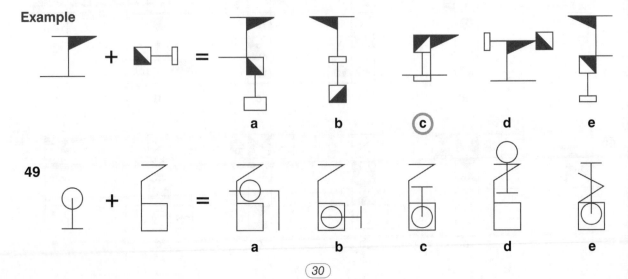

49

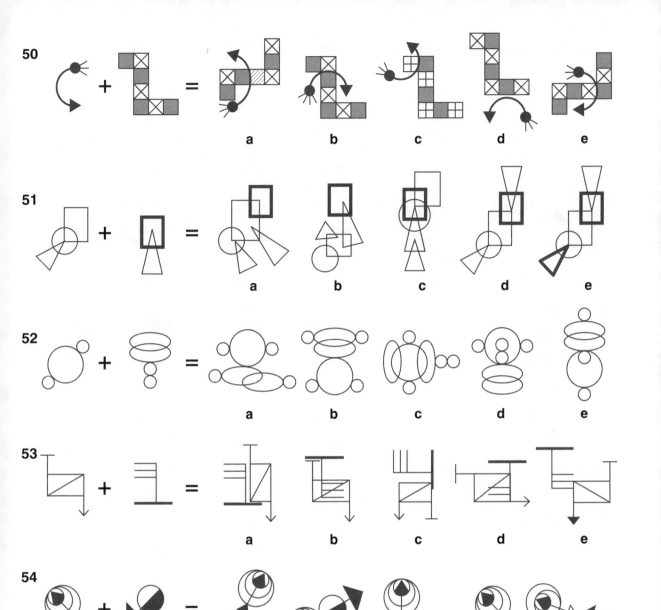

Which shape on the right is the reflection of the shape given on the left? Circle the letter.

Example

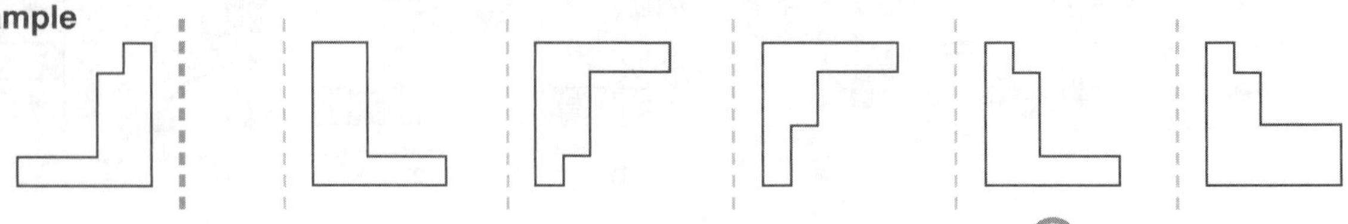

a   b   c   (d)   e

55

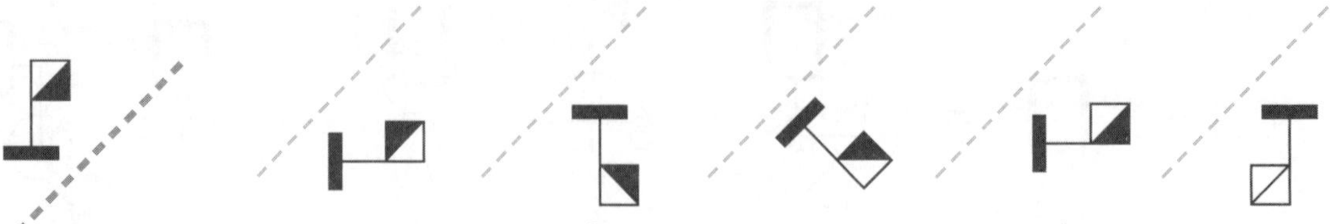

a   b   c   d   e

56

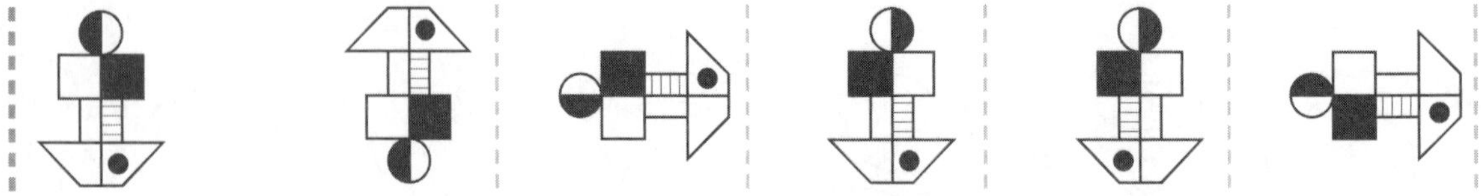

a   b   c   d   e

57

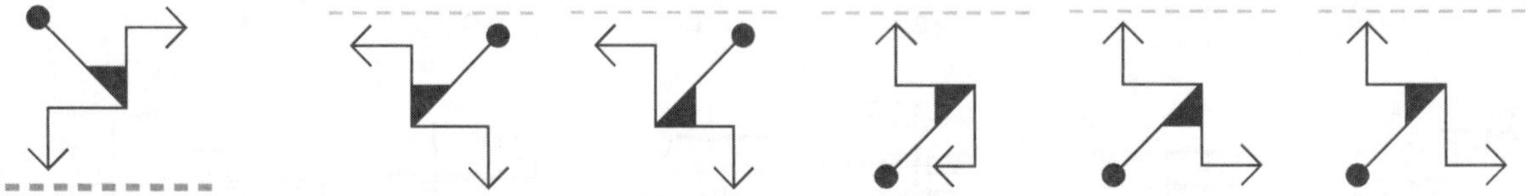

a   b   c   d   e

58

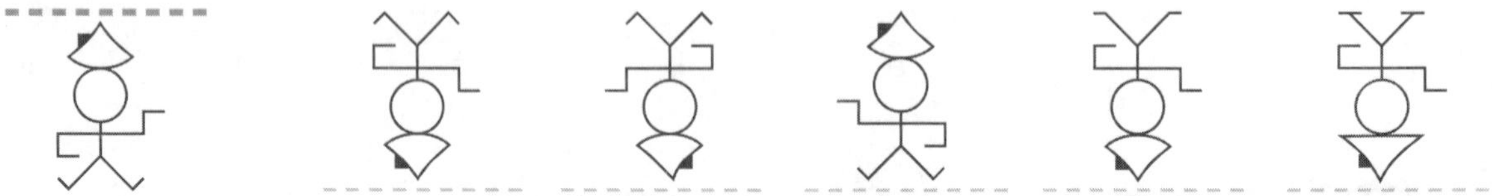

a   b   c   d   e

59

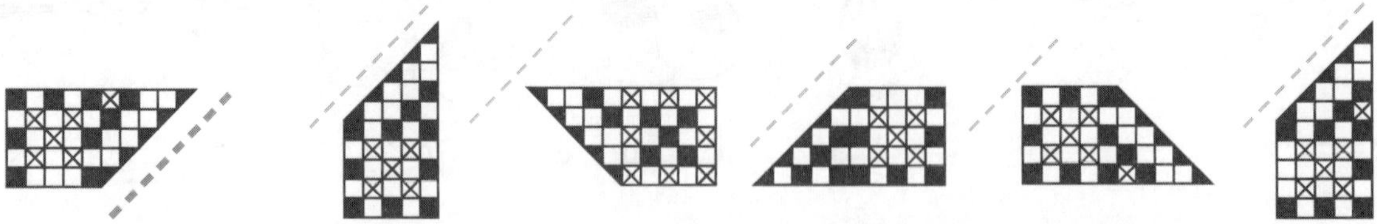

a   b   c   d   e

60

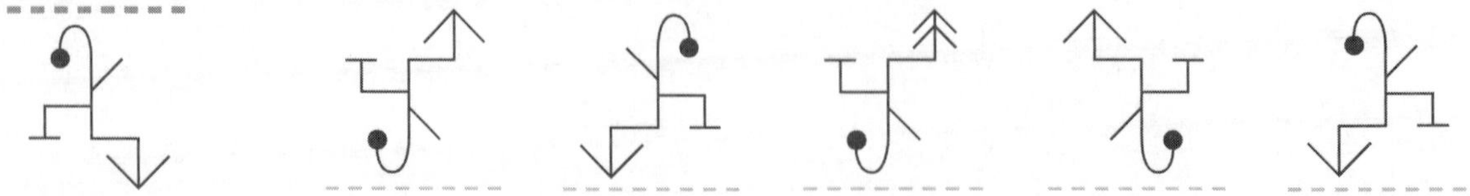

a   b   c   d   e

Paper 1

1 a		**31** c	
2 c		**32** d	
3 c		**33** e	
4 a		**34** b	
5 b		**35** e	
6 d		**36** e	
7 a		**37** e	
8 d		**38** b	
9 e		**39** c	
10 c		**40** c	
11 a		**41** b	
12 b		**42** c	
13 d		**43** c	
14 e		**44** e	
15 e		**45** b	
16 b		**46** d	
17 c		**47** d	
18 d		**48** d	
19 c		**49** e	
20 d		**50** c	
21 d		**51** e	
22 e		**52** e	
23 b		**53** c	
24 e		**54** d	
25 d		**55** c	
26 a		**56** a	
27 d		**57** e	
28 e		**58** d	
29 c		**59** e	
30 d		**60** d	

Paper 2

1 d		**31** d	
2 c		**32** a	
3 e		**33** e	
4 d		**34** c	
5 e		**35** e	
6 e		**36** e	
7 d		**37** d	
8 c		**38** e	
9 b		**39** d	
10 e		**40** c	
11 e		**41** d	
12 d		**42** e	
13 e		**43** c	
14 d		**44** d	
15 e		**45** e	
16 b		**46** d	
17 b		**47** b	
18 c		**48** e	
19 c		**49** c	
20 d		**50** d	
21 c		**51** e	
22 d		**52** e	
23 c		**53** c	
24 d		**54** c	
25 e		**55** e	
26 b		**56** e	
27 e		**57** c	
28 d		**58** d	
29 e		**59** e	
30 a		**60** d	

Paper 3

1	d	31	b
2	e	32	d
3	e	33	e
4	c	34	d
5	c	35	b
6	e	36	e
7	b	37	d
8	e	38	c
9	c	39	e
10	d	40	b
11	c	41	d
12	c	42	c
13	d	43	d
14	c	44	d
15	c	45	d
16	d	46	d
17	e	47	b
18	e	48	b
19	b	49	c
20	c	50	e
21	e	51	d
22	d	52	d
23	e	53	b
24	e	54	c
25	e	55	a
26	c	56	d
27	e	57	d
28	b	58	a
29	e	59	e
30	e	60	a

Paper 4

1	e	31	e
2	b	32	b
3	e	33	e
4	c	34	d
5	b	35	d
6	c	36	b
7	c	37	b
8	d	38	d
9	a	39	d
10	d	40	e
11	d	41	b
12	d	42	c
13	d	43	c
14	c	44	e
15	e	45	c
16	d	46	c
17	e	47	a
18	d	48	d
19	c	49	a
20	b	50	e
21	d	51	b
22	a	52	d
23	d	53	a
24	a	54	d
25	e	55	a
26	e	56	c
27	b	57	d
28	b	58	c
29	c	59	e
30	e	60	d

1 e	31 d	1 e	31 c
2 b	32 c	2 c	32 e
3 c	33 e	3 b	33 d
4 b	34 e	4 d	34 d
5 d	35 e	5 b	35 b
6 e	36 c	6 e	36 e
7 c	37 d	7 d	37 d
8 d	38 c	8 e	38 c
9 e	39 e	9 d	39 c
10 d	40 c	10 c	40 a
11 c	41 c	11 b	41 e
12 e	42 c	12 d	42 c
13 e	43 e	13 d	43 d
14 c	44 c	14 e	44 c
15 d	45 e	15 d	45 e
16 e	46 c	16 c	46 b
17 d	47 e	17 b	47 e
18 c	48 b	18 e	48 b
19 d	49 d	19 e	49 e
20 c	50 e	20 b	50 a
21 e	51 b	21 d	51 c
22 e	52 c	22 c	52 d
23 c	53 a	23 a	53 c
24 e	54 c	24 e	54 b
25 a	55 d	25 e	55 d
26 e	56 e	26 c	56 d
27 b	57 d	27 c	57 c
28 d	58 d	28 d	58 e
29 e	59 b	29 d	59 e
30 d	60 c	30 e	60 c

Paper 4

Which pattern on the right belongs in the group on the left? Circle the letter.

Example

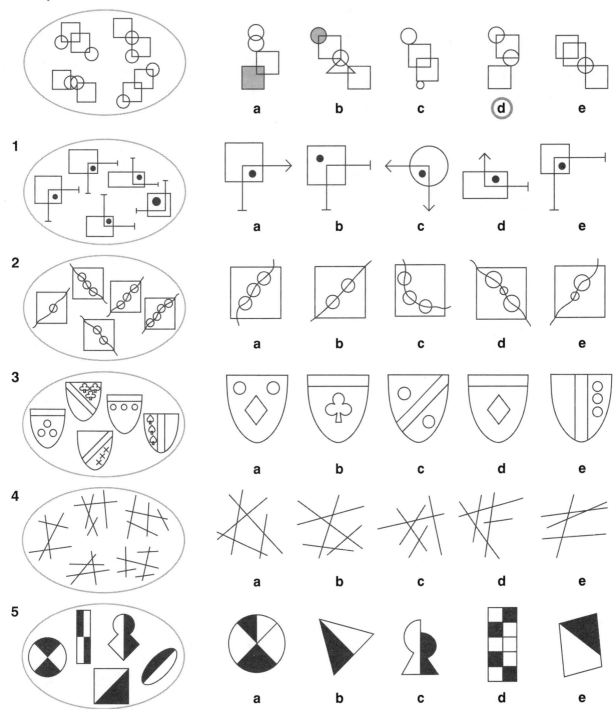

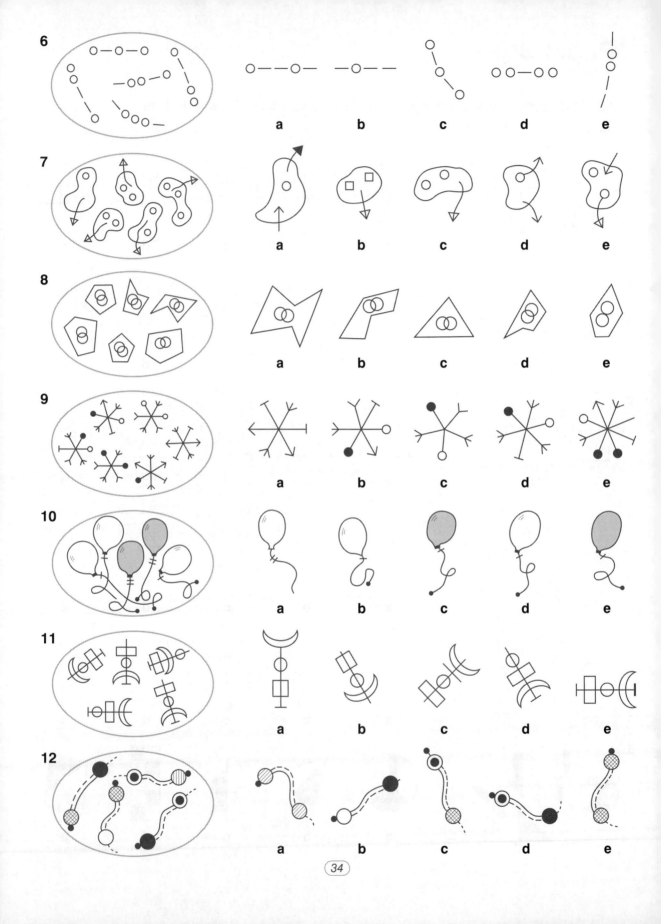

Which one comes next? Circle the letter.

Example

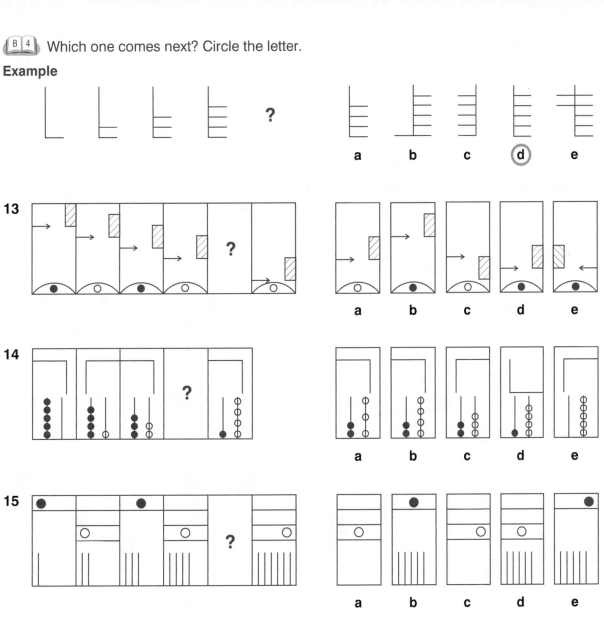

13

14

15

16

17

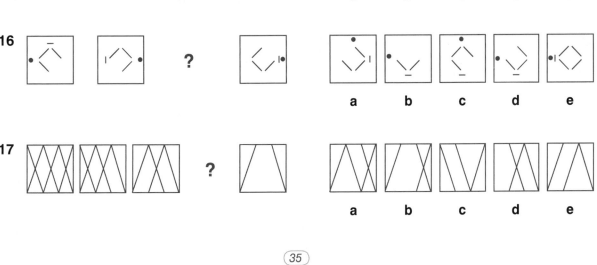

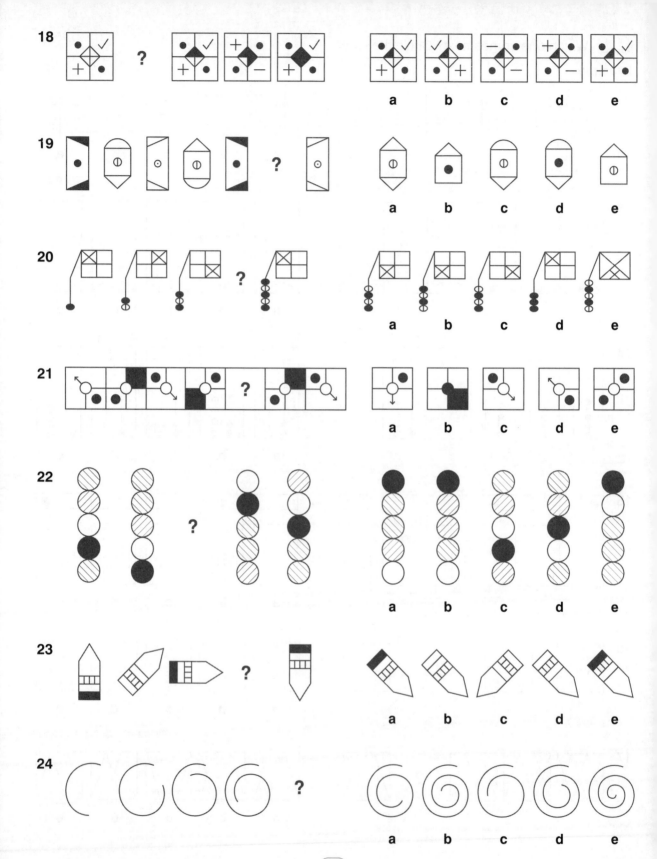

18

19

20

21

22

23

24

a b c d e

Which shape or pattern on the right completes the second pair in the same way as the first pair? Circle the letter.

Example

is to ... as ... is to

       a   **b**   **c**   **(d)**   **e**

25 is to ... as ... is to

       a   **b**   **c**   **d**   **e**

26 is to ... as ... is to

       a   **b**   **c**   **d**   **e**

27 is to ... as ... is to

       a   **b**   **c**   **d**   **e**

28 is to ... as ... is to

       a   **b**   **c**   **d**   **e**

29 is to ... as ... is to

       a   **b**   **c**   **d**   **e**

30 is to ... as ... is to

       a   **b**   **c**   **d**   **e**

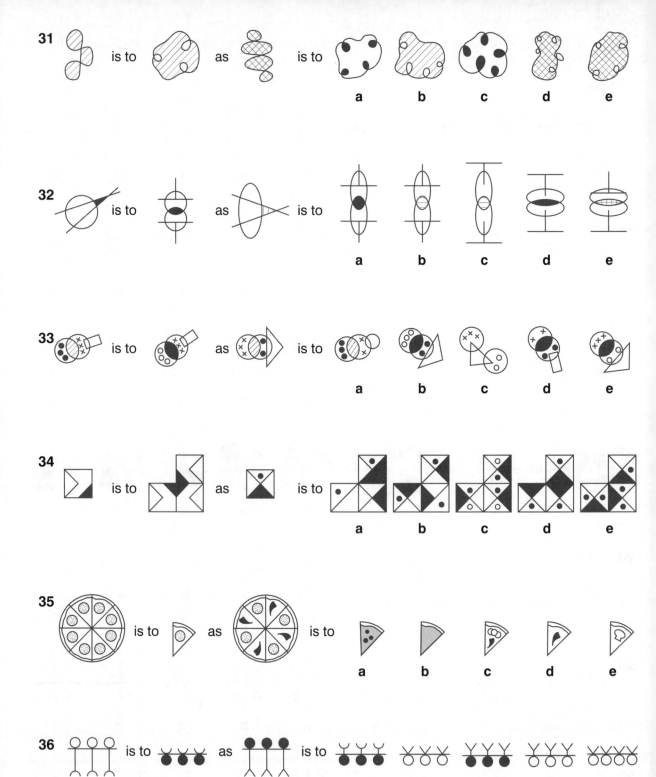

31

32

33

34

35

36

a   b   c   d   e

Which code matches the shape or pattern given at the end of each line?
Circle the letter.

Example

AX   AY   BZ   CY   BX   ?

	BZ	AZ	CX	BY	CZ
	a	b	c	d	(e)

37

GZ   HZ   GY   HX   IX   IY   ?

	HY	IZ	GX	IY	GZ
	a	b	c	d	e

38

EL   FN   GL   EM   GN   FM   ?

	GL	FM	EL	GM	FL
	a	b	c	d	e

39

BP   DQ   CR   AR   BS   DP   ?

	AS	BR	CP	AQ	DS
	a	b	c	d	e

40

LF   LE   ME   ND   OD   ?

	LD	MF	MD	NE	NF
	a	b	c	d	e

41

XC   YB   ZE   XD   ZC   ?

	XE	YD	ZD	YE	ZB
	a	b	c	d	e

42

CY   BZ   AY   AZ   CX   ?

	AX	CZ	BX	BY	CX
	a	b	c	d	e

B8 Which cube can be made from the given net? Circle the letter.

Example

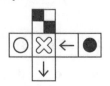

   a   **b**   **c**   **d**   **e**

43
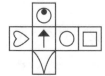

   a   **b**   **c**   **d**   **e**

44
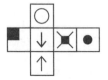

   a   **b**   **c**   **d**   **e**

45
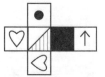

   a   **b**   **c**   **d**   **e**

46
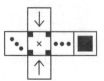

   a   **b**   **c**   **d**   **e**

47
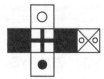

   a   **b**   **c**   **d**   **e**

48
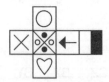

   a   **b**   **c**   **d**   **e**

B 7 Which shape on the right is the reflection of the shape given on the left? Circle the letter.

Example

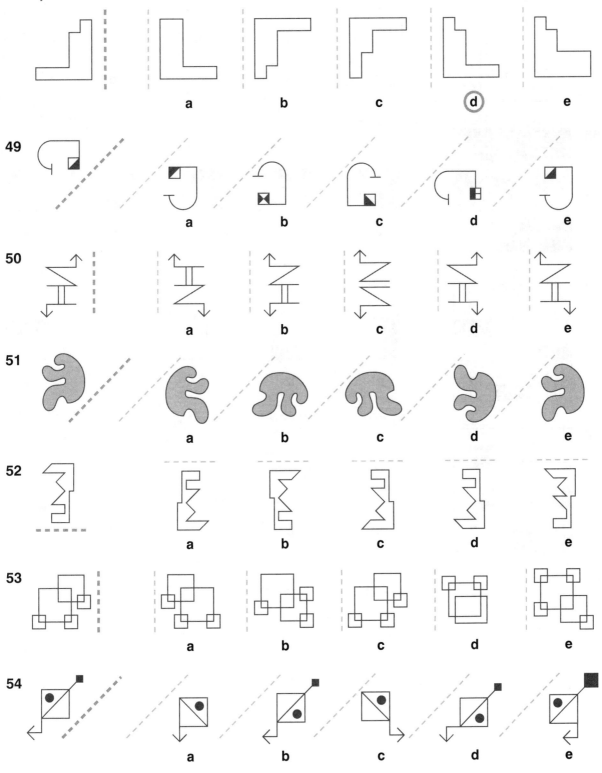

Which shape or pattern completes the larger square? Circle the letter.

Example

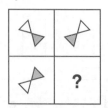

a   b   c   (d)   e

55

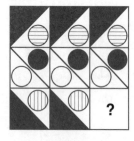

a   b   c   d   e

56

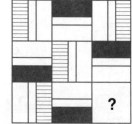

a   b   c   d   e

57

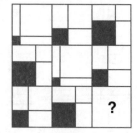

a   b   c   d   e

58

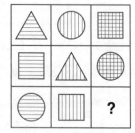

a   b   c   d   e

59

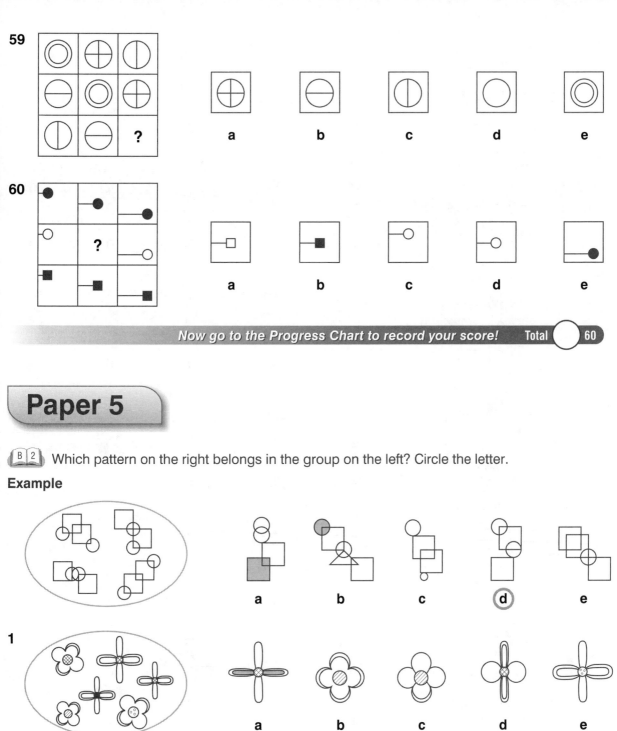

a   b   c   d   e

60

a   b   c   d   e

Now go to the Progress Chart to record your score!   Total ◯ 60

Paper 5

B 2 Which pattern on the right belongs in the group on the left? Circle the letter.

Example

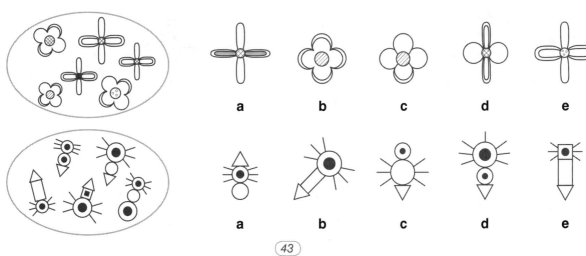

a   b   c   (d)   e

1

a   b   c   d   e

2

a   b   c   d   e

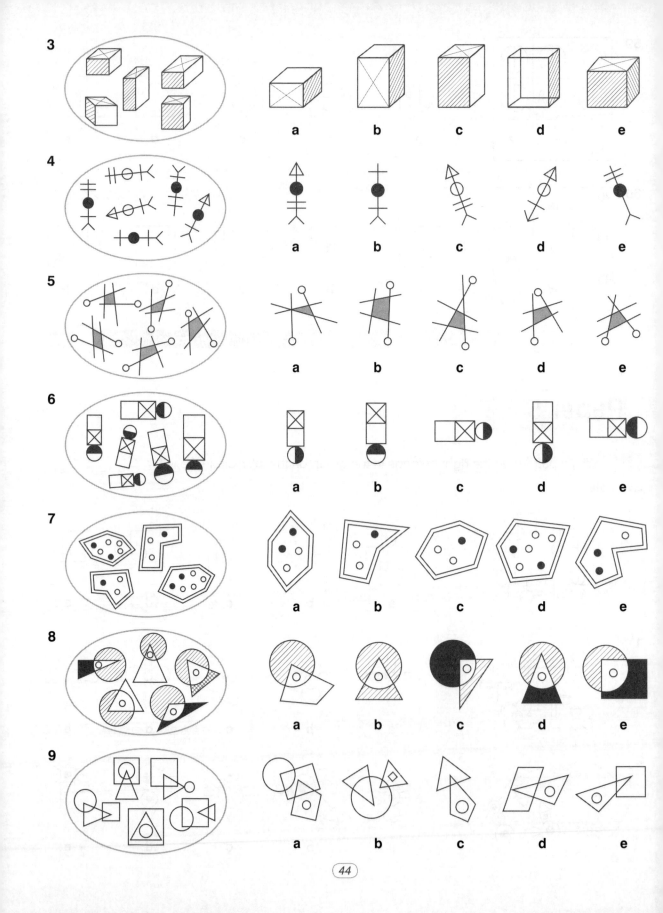

3

a   b   c   d   e

4

a   b   c   d   e

5

a   b   c   d   e

6

a   b   c   d   e

7

a   b   c   d   e

8

a   b   c   d   e

9

a   b   c   d   e

44

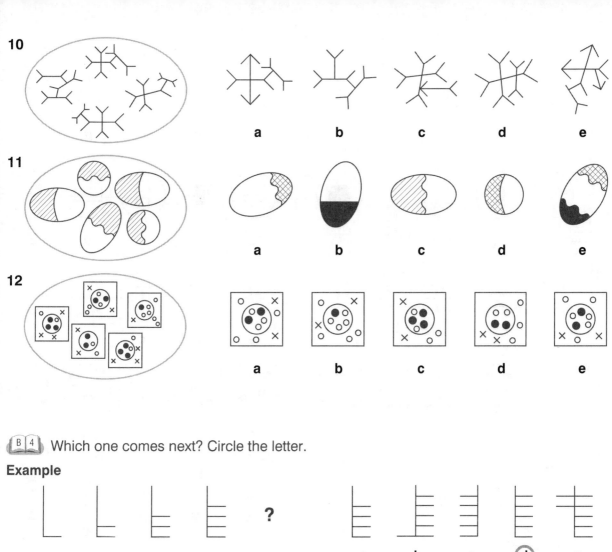

10

11

12

Which one comes next? Circle the letter.

Example

? a b c d e

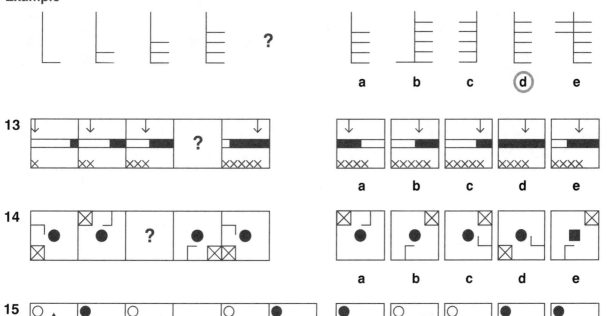

13

a b c d e

14

a b c d e

15

a b c d e

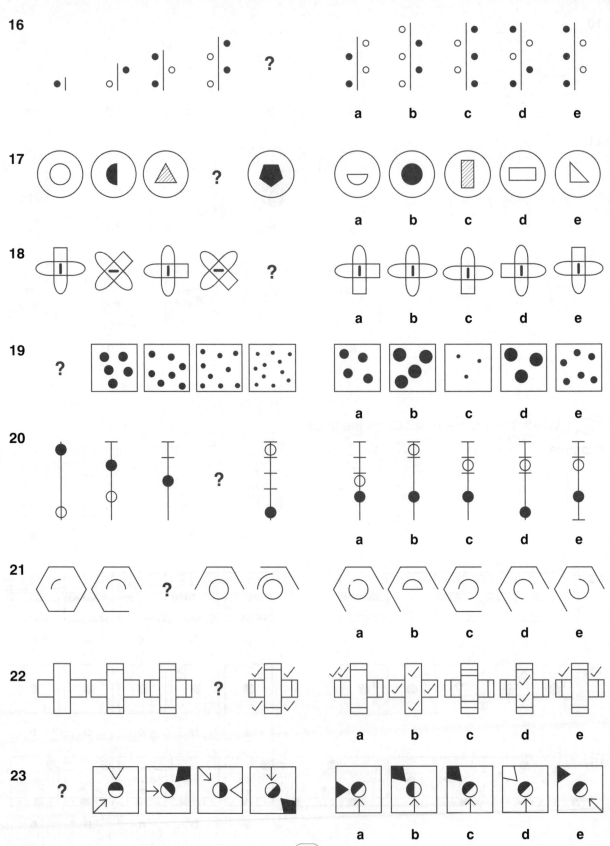

16

a b c d e

17

a b c d e

18

a b c d e

19

a b c d e

20

a b c d e

21

a b c d e

22

a b c d e

23

a b c d e

24

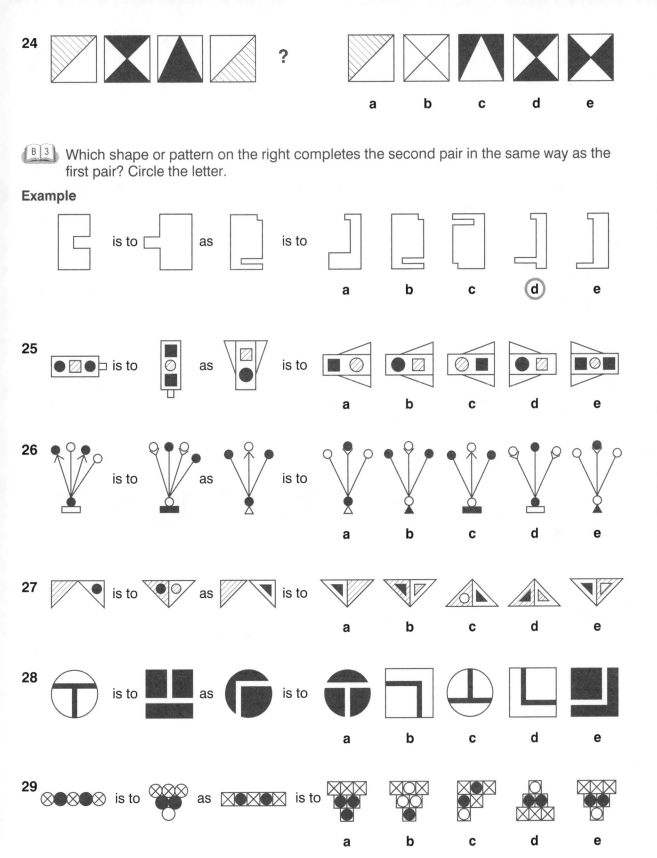

a   b   c   d   e

B 3 Which shape or pattern on the right completes the second pair in the same way as the first pair? Circle the letter.

Example

is to   as   is to

a   b   c   (d)   e

25

is to   as   is to

a   b   c   d   e

26

is to   as   is to

a   b   c   d   e

27

is to   as   is to

a   b   c   d   e

28

is to   as   is to

a   b   c   d   e

29

is to   as   is to

a   b   c   d   e

47

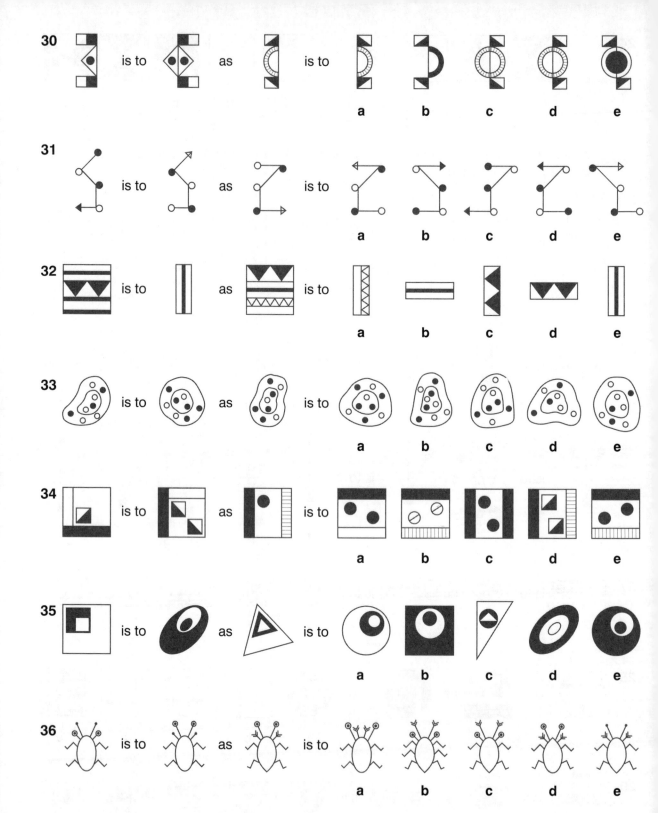

B 9 Which code matches the shape or pattern given at the end of each line?
Circle the letter.

Example

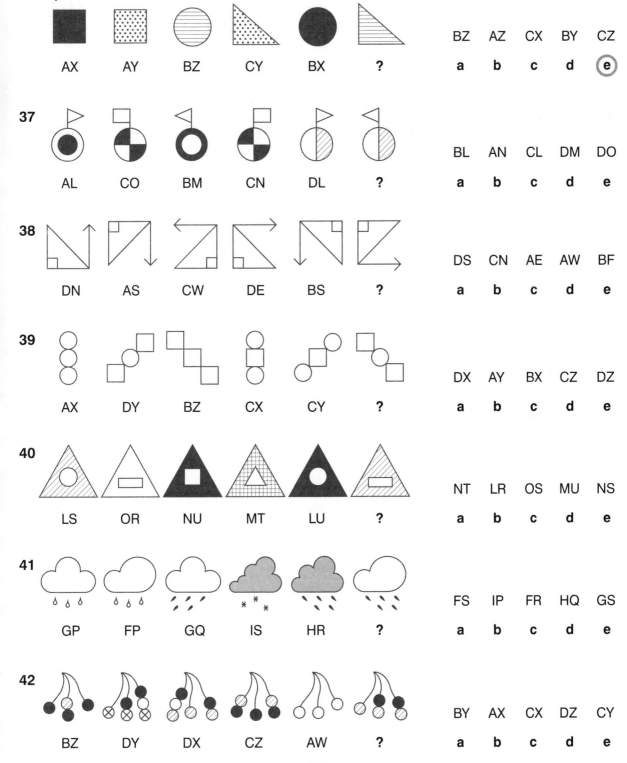

	BZ	AZ	CX	BY	CZ
AX AY BZ CY BX **?**	a	b	c	d	ⓔ

37

	BL	AN	CL	DM	DO
AL CO BM CN DL **?**	a	b	c	d	e

38

	DS	CN	AE	AW	BF
DN AS CW DE BS **?**	a	b	c	d	e

39

	DX	AY	BX	CZ	DZ
AX DY BZ CX CY **?**	a	b	c	d	e

40

	NT	LR	OS	MU	NS
LS OR NU MT LU **?**	a	b	c	d	e

41

	FS	IP	FR	HQ	GS
GP FP GQ IS HR **?**	a	b	c	d	e

42

	BY	AX	CX	DZ	CY
BZ DY DX CZ AW **?**	a	b	c	d	e

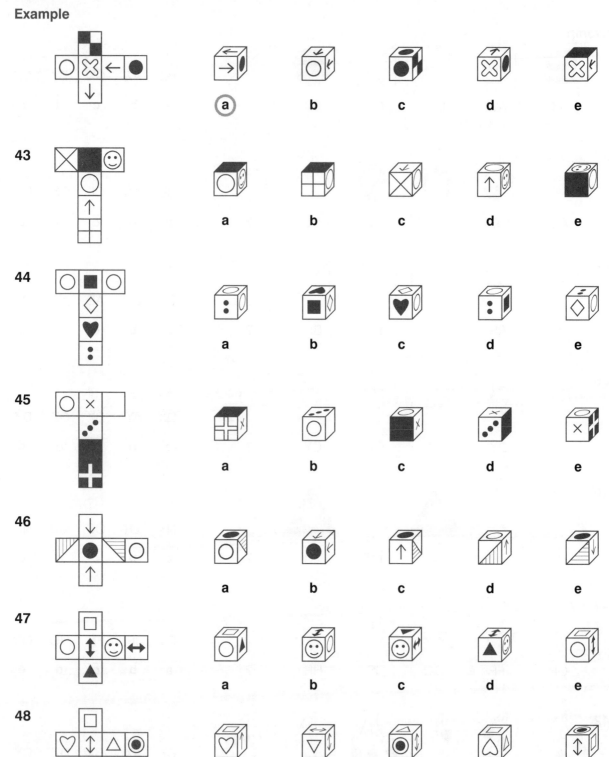

B 8 Which cube can be made from the given net? Circle the letter.

Example

a   b   c   d   e

43

a   b   c   d   e

44

a   b   c   d   e

45

a   b   c   d   e

46

a   b   c   d   e

47

a   b   c   d   e

48

a   b   c   d   e

Which shape on the right is the reflection of the shape given on the left? Circle the letter.

Example

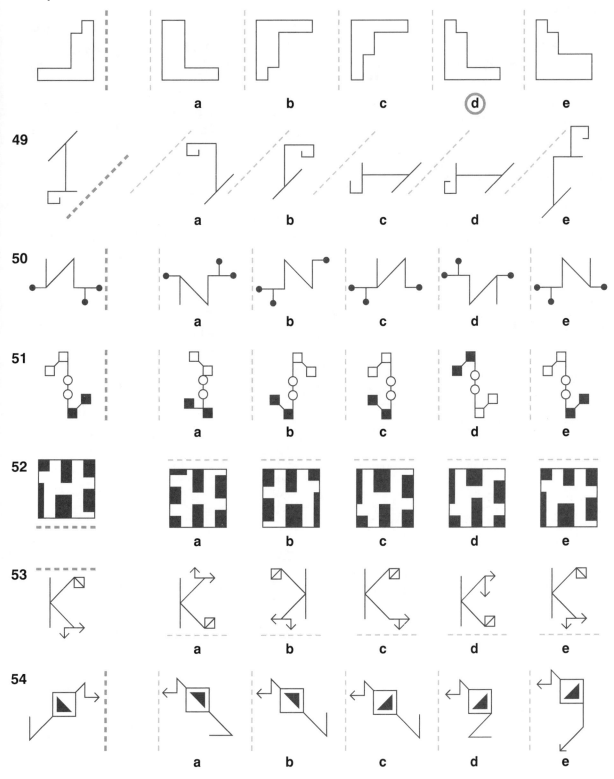

49

50

51

52

53

54

Which shape or pattern is made when the first two shapes or patterns are put together? Circle the letter.

Example

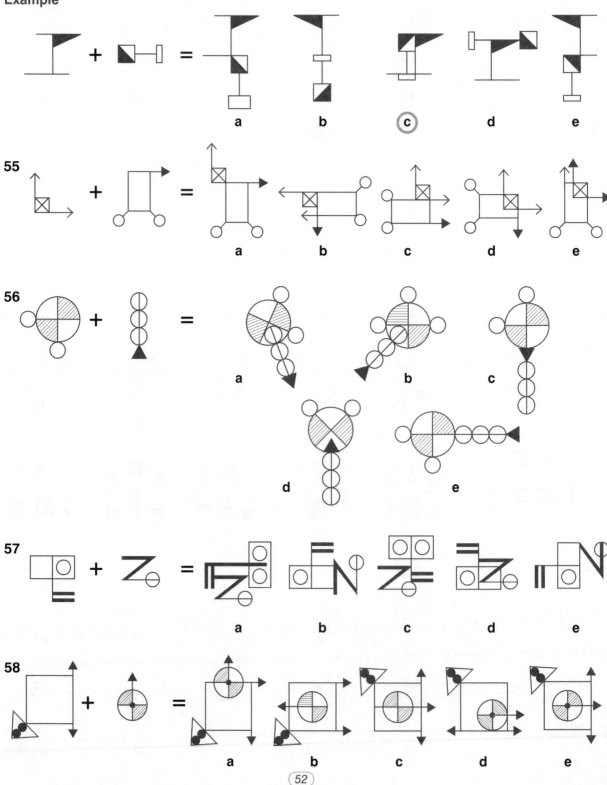

55

56

57

58

59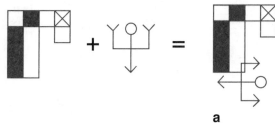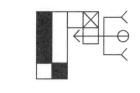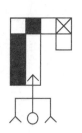

a b c d e

60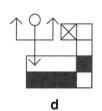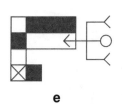

a b c

d e

Paper 6

B 2 Which pattern on the right belongs in the group on the left? Circle the letter.

Example

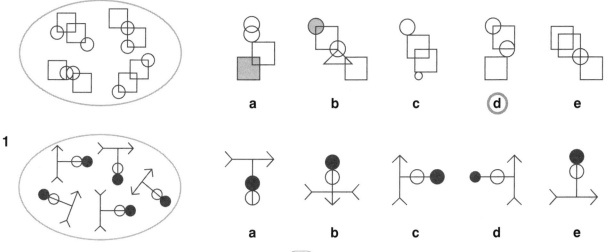

a b c d e

1

a b c d e

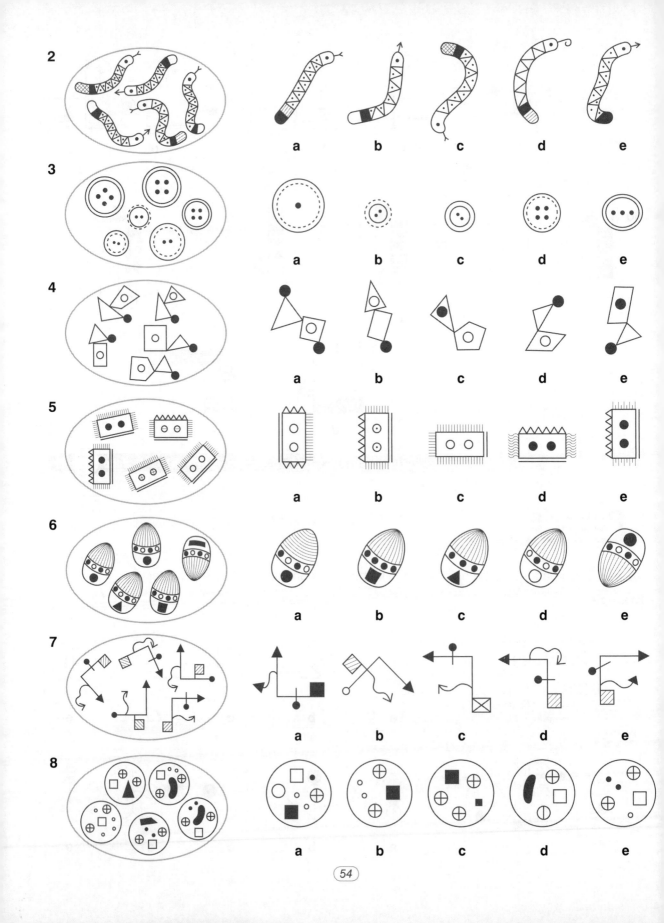

9

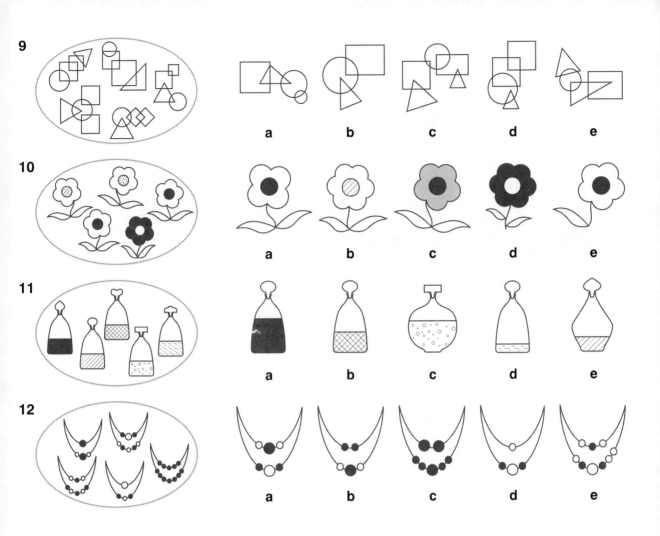

a   b   c   d   e

10

a   b   c   d   e

11

a   b   c   d   e

12

a   b   c   d   e

B 4 Which one comes next? Circle the letter.

Example

a   b   c   d   e

13

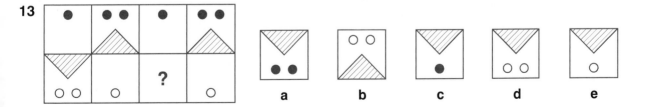

a   b   c   d   e

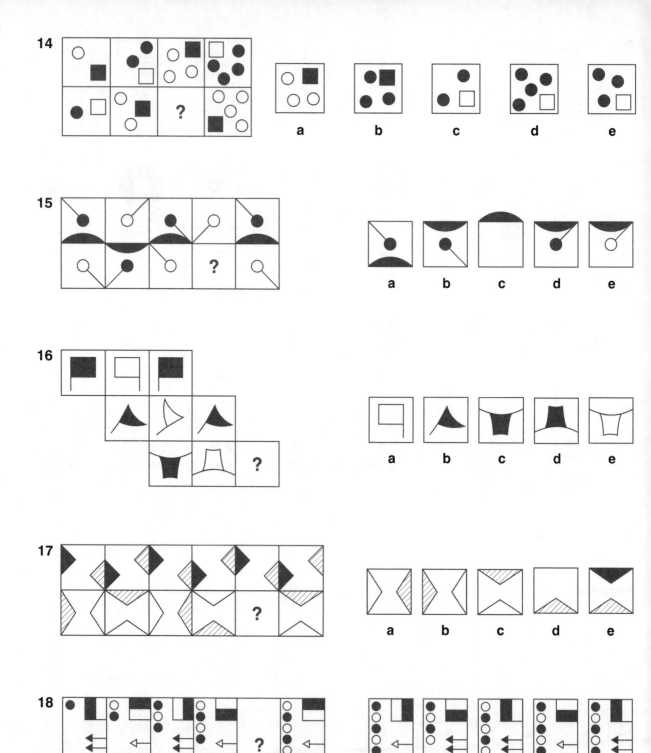

Which shape or pattern on the right completes the second pair in the same way as the first pair? Circle the letter.

Example

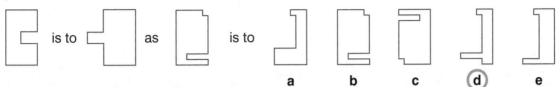

                                               a   **b**   **c**   **(d)**   **e**

19 is to as is to

                                               a   **b**   **c**   **d**   **e**

20 is to as is to

                                               a   **b**   **c**   **d**   **e**

21 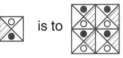 is to as is to

                                               a   **b**   **c**   **d**   **e**

22 is to as is to

                                               a   **b**   **c**   **d**   **e**

23 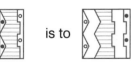 is to  as is to

                                               a   **b**   **c**   **d**   **e**

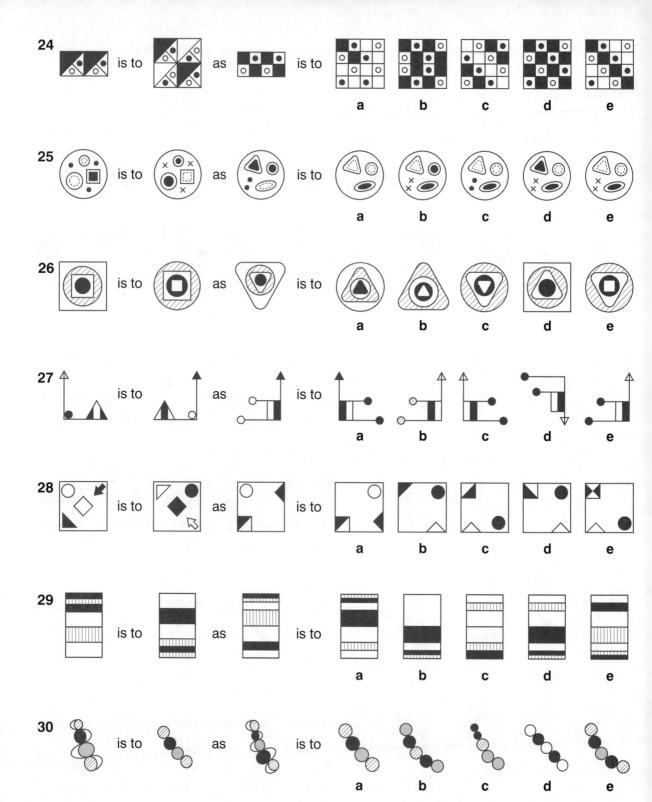

Which code matches the shape or pattern given at the end of each line?
Circle the letter.

Example

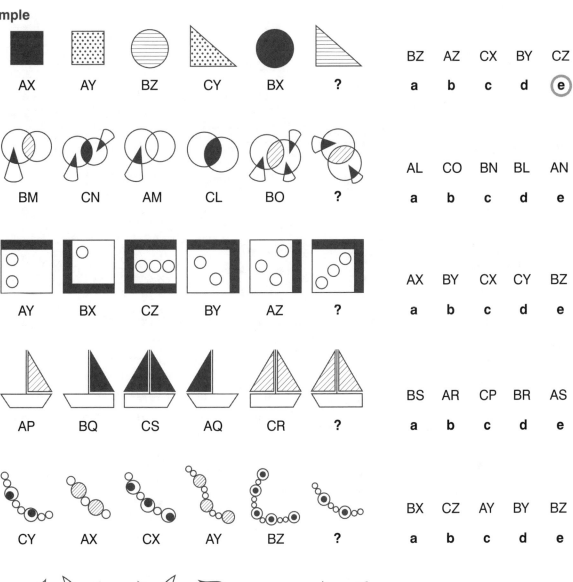

						BZ	AZ	CX	BY	CZ
AX	AY	BZ	CY	BX	?	a	b	c	d	(e)

31

						AL	CO	BN	BL	AN
BM	CN	AM	CL	BO	?	a	b	c	d	e

32

						AX	BY	CX	CY	BZ
AY	BX	CZ	BY	AZ	?	a	b	c	d	e

33

						BS	AR	CP	BR	AS
AP	BQ	CS	AQ	CR	?	a	b	c	d	e

34

						BX	CZ	AY	BY	BZ
CY	AX	CX	AY	BZ	?	a	b	c	d	e

35

						AS	CU	CT	BS	CV
AT	BU	AV	CS	BT	?	a	b	c	d	e

36

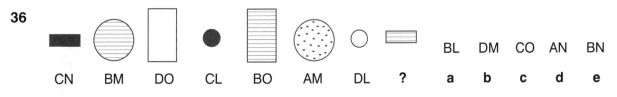

								BL	DM	CO	AN	BN
CN	BM	DO	CL	BO	AM	DL	?	a	b	c	d	e

Which is the odd one out? Circle the letter.

Example

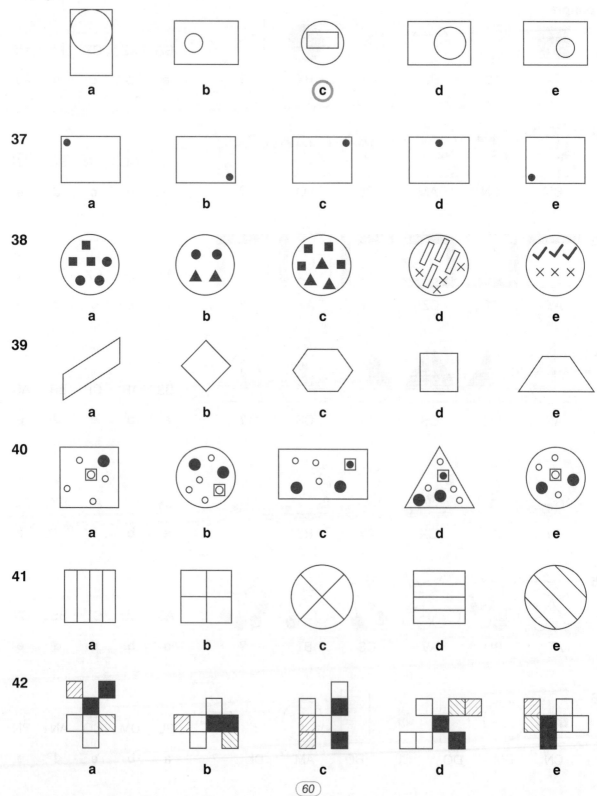

Which net makes the cube? Circle the letter.

Example

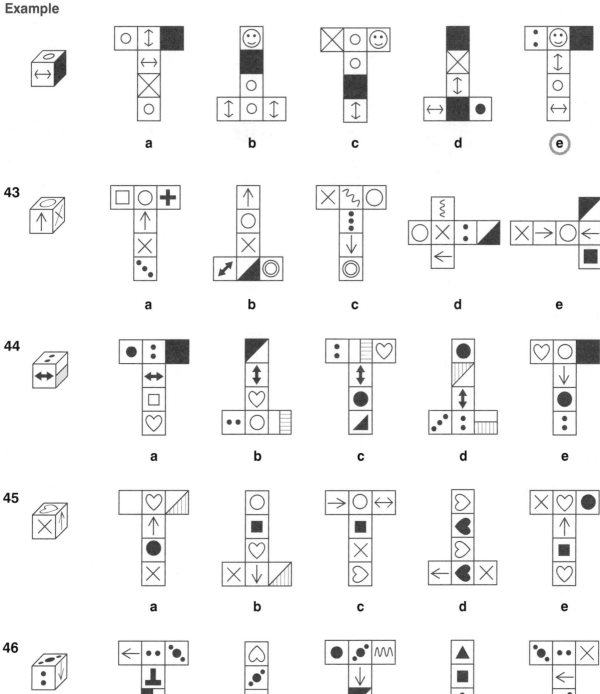

a   b   c   d   e

43

a   b   c   d   e

44

a   b   c   d   e

45

a   b   c   d   e

46

a   b   c   d   e

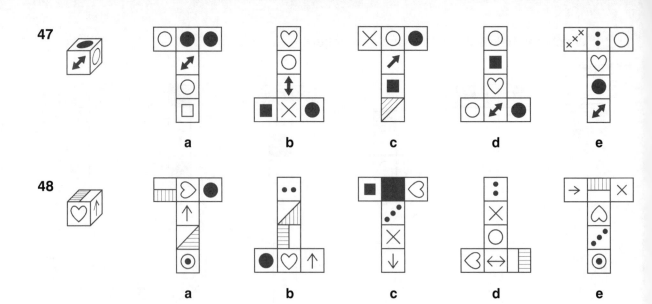

47   a   b   c   d   e

48   a   b   c   d   e

B 7 Which shape on the right is the reflection of the shape given on the left? Circle the letter.

Example

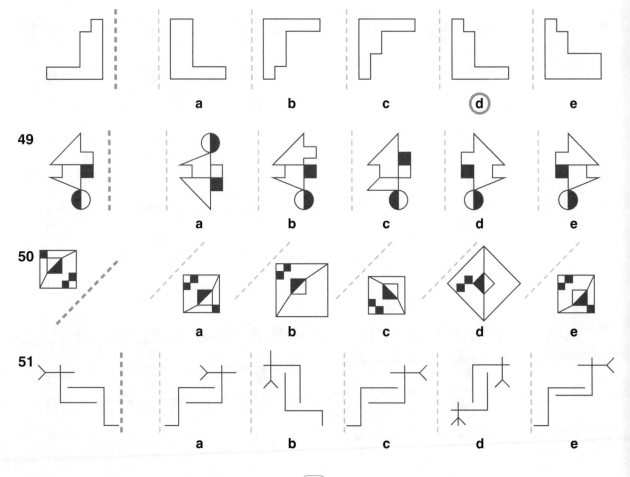

49

50

51

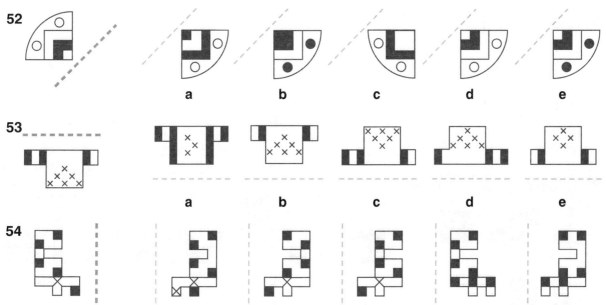

52
a   b   c   d   e

53
a   b   c   d   e

54
a   b   c   d   e

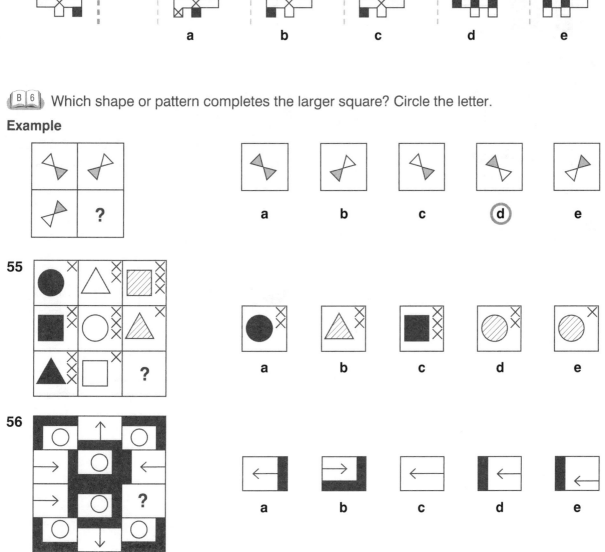

B 6 Which shape or pattern completes the larger square? Circle the letter.

Example

a   b   c   **d**   e

55

a   b   c   d   e

56

a   b   c   d   e

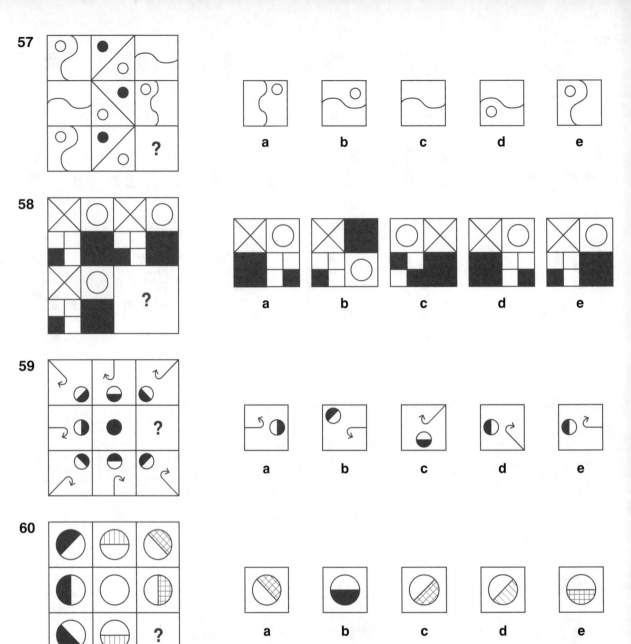

Now go to the Progress Chart to record your score!   Total   60

64

Progress Chart   Non-verbal Reasoning 11$^+$–12$^+$ years Book 1

Total marks	Paper 1	Paper 2	Paper 3	Paper 4	Paper 5	Paper 6	Percentage
60							100%
57							
54							90%
51							85%
48							80%
45							
42							70%
39							
36							60%
33							
30							50%
27							
24							40%
21							
18							30%
15							
12							20%
9							
6							10%
3							
0	1	2	3	4	5	6	0%

Date ▶

When you've finished the book use the Next Step Planner ➡